ANXIETY + DEPRESSION

Effective Treatment
of the Big Two
Co-Occurring Disorders

MARGARET WEHRENBERG

W. W. NORTON & COMPANY

NEW YORK | LONDON

For information about permission to reproduce selections from this book, write to Permissions, W. W. Norton & Company, Inc., 500 Fifth Avenue, New York, NY 10110

For information about special discounts for bulk purchases, please contact W. W. Norton Special Sales at specialsales@wwnorton.com or 800-233-4830

Manufacturing by Courier Westford
Production manager: Leeann Graham

Library of Congress Cataloging-in-Publication Data

Wehrenberg, Margaret.
  Anxiety + depression : effective treatment of the big two co-occurring disorders / Margaret Wehrenberg. — First edition.
    pages cm
  "A Norton professional book."
  Includes bibliographical references and index.
  ISBN 978-0-393-70873-8 (hardcover)
  1. Anxiety—Treatment. 2. Depression, Mental—Treatment.
  3. Comorbidity. I. Title. II. Title: Anxiety and depression.
  RC531.W424 2014
  616.85'22—dc23
                  2013049976

W. W. Norton & Company, Inc.
500 Fifth Avenue, New York, N.Y. 10110
www.wwnorton.com

W. W. Norton & Company Ltd.
Castle House, 75/76 Wells Street, London W1T 3QT

1 2 3 4 5 6 7 8 9 0

For the many people
with whom I've been privileged
to work over these many years.

Contents

Acknowledgments

GETTING A book into print is never a solo task, and I am very appreciative of those people who helped me along the way on this one. First, I am deeply grateful to Andrea Dawson, my editor, who encouraged me to write about my experiences with clients who suffer anxiety and depression. She was a central force in the conceptualization of this work and also in the structure of the book. I would not have managed it without her excellent advice and appropriately-timed nudging. My copy editor, Casey Ruble, is another whose work to polish my words was necessary and is unparalleled. She has an uncanny knack of writing in my voice so that whatever she adds to flow of the manuscript comes out as if my inner better writer produced it.

I also get by with a little help from my friends. When I am in the throes of writing, I don't give them the attention they deserve and still they offer so much support. Cathy Lessmann is my wonderful local voice of cheer, ready to offer me dinner, and a reminder to get outside. Shannon Burns makes space for me both literally and emotionally, and Susan Palo Cherwien expands my knowledge as she shares her own, and she never fails to make me feel valued. There are *many* (everyone should blessed) who add such pleasure and positivity to my life that I can continue to work with my clients with joy and energy.

Introduction

Co-occurring anxiety and depression are not always obvious—even to a seasoned therapist. It has happened to me more than once: I see a client for anxiety and decide a psychiatric consult regarding med ication is in order. The client comes back with a diagnosis of depression and, of course, a prescription for medication to treat the depression but no mention of the anxiety I thought was the problem. Now there are two professionals with two views of the same symptoms. Who is right? I suspect that, most of the time, we both are. Herein lies the challenge: It's hard enough to treat these disorders when they exist on their own, and it gets even harder when they present together.

The biggest challenge is being able to spot both problems. Typically one symptom picture dominates, at least in the description we obtain from clients. But think about some of the obvious ways these two disorders interact:

- A person who is depressed and very low on energy may not have the mental "oomph" to fight constant anxious rumina-tion, and the anxiety will make depression worse.
- When acute anxiety is unremitting and uncontrolled, it can make any person depressed and exhausted.

- A high-energy client who complains of constant worry may not recognize how the depressive feelings of pessimism and inadequacy are leading to the worry about failing or making mistakes. Symptom management of worry will be less effective if the depression isn't also treated.
- A quiet, shy client who has become socially anxious may become depressed as the social anxiety leads to avoidance of activities that might have interested him or her. The depression makes it harder to have motivation to overcome social fear and reengage with others.

Even when you *can* see that both disorders are present, how do you know where to start in therapy?

As a clinician specializing in anxiety and depression, and with more than 30 years of experience, I have seen the challenges that these two co-occurring (comorbid) conditions produce. They appear together so often that we need to ask some questions:

- How common is this comorbidity and why does it exist?
- How can I be sure my client is showing signs of *both* anxiety and depression? What indications of comorbidity should I look for?
- Is there a way to identify when one disorder is more prominent than the other? If so, do I treat one first and then the other? If not, should I view them as the same clinical problem, and treat both in tandem?
- How will one disorder affect treatment response when I work with the other?

Consider the following case:

Pat sought help for what she said was overwhelming anxiety. She reported that she constantly fretted about her health and her husband's health. (Neither was sick, but they could be!) She worried about whether she had offended someone, berated herself for having been so stupid as to buy a house in a neighborhood with so many noisy children, and was concerned that she would be fired for working too slowly, despite the fact that her boss had never voiced such a complaint. She worried about whether she would lose her friends because she worried so much.

What were hard to see, and what Pat did not recognize either, were the common themes of loss and failure underlying her anxiety. In fact, she had strong feelings of worthlessness and hopelessness about the future (symptoms of depression) that had to be addressed if she was to feel less anxious. In this way, the depression Pat did not identify would interfere with letting go of worry, and it needed to be addressed to successfully diminish her anxiety.

Conversely, sometimes an underlying anxiety fuels depression. This was the case with Mark.

Mark told me he didn't know how much longer he could pretend to be working before the others in his office caught on. He said that he tried to work but couldn't concentrate and felt sluggish and unmotivated. At the end of the day he went straight home to lie on the couch all evening. Mark presented as depressed. But a fuller picture developed when I began asking him about how he had functioned previously. Mark reported that he had always been a worrier, and he so annoyed his wife with requests for reassurance that she finally left him, not wanting to be married to such a "clingy" man and feel so responsible for his wellbeing. The anxiety that had plagued Mark eventually turned into depression, partly as a result of the losses he had suffered and partly because of his inability to handle anxiety. Mark had never had a particularly positive outlook on life, but the persistent, nagging doubt and anxiety completely squashed any natural optimism he might have had otherwise.

These kinds of clients walk into your clinical office every week. This book describes the most frequently seen combinations of anxiety and depression and explains how these two disorders affect each other as the client moves through the process of therapy.

Although the methods I use to help clients manage and eliminate symptoms are grounded in solid clinical research and supported in the literature on how therapies work, the interplay I describe is based on my own extensive experience with clients who suffer from depression and anxiety. I will address questions I frequently hear from therapists when I teach seminars. For example:

> *"I have a client whom I thought had generalized anxiety— lots of worry, strong physical agitation. But I see her as having no joy or optimism. I thought that would clear up as she managed her worry better, but I don't see it getting any better. Is it possible she is depressed?"*

My answer: "Most definitely!" In this book, I will describe how that kind of depression can masquerade as acute anxiety and discuss how it undermines the client's attempts to manage anxiety. Treatment methods must interweave depression management with anxiety treatment; if they don't, the client will become depressed about lack of progress, too.

> *"I'm treating a 50-year-old man who says he has been depressed since his wife died. He seems to have dealt with his grief, but he still*

has no zest for life, and he is wondering what the future will hold. He doesn't know how to connect with neighbors and has no friendships outside of talking to people at work. Could he possibly be anxious about meeting new people or going into social situations without his wife? Could I be missing social anxiety?"

Yes, of course. Life experiences such as the death of a loved one do not always result in depression, but they can when the circumstances of a person's life are dramatically altered and the person does not have the skills to cope with it. A socially anxious (or panicky) person may come to rely on a family member and never see the anxiety as an impediment until life forces him or her to function alone.

"Is there any way to definitively rule out anxiety or depression?"

That is a question that has to be answered equivocally. Although there are assessment tools that effectively measure the degree of anxiety or depression, like the Beck or Hamilton scales so popular in research studies, the symptoms on these scales are not mutually exclusive: A person can have high scores on scales for both anxiety and depression. Ideas about how to parse what disorder is dominant and how each affects the other are the meat of this book.

"Are these disorders one and the same, with varying dominant symptoms?"

We might end up deciding that is the case at some point in the future, but I suspect it's an issue of underlying neurobiology intersecting with life experience to push the client toward depression or anxiety. In my clinical practice, I spend a fair amount of time looking for signs of biology of depression or anxiety that preexisted the life situation that catapulted the client into anxiety or depression, and I've found that certain life circumstances, like trauma, often push clients toward anxiety whereas other circumstances, like significant losses, push clients more toward depression.

"Isn't it necessary to get at underlying causes before you can effectively treat the anxiety or depression regardless of which seems dominant?"

For many reasons, which I will outline in different cases, symptom treatment can be effective and often leads clients to recognize that there is some underlying cause of their symptoms, such as growing up with an abusive parent or addicted family member. When clients have effective treatment for the symptoms of anxiety or depression, they are equipped with skills to manage the anxiety-provoking aspects of treatment for underlying issues. They are also more ready for the emotional challenges of dealing with the underlying causes.

"When the diagnosis becomes clear, how do I decide what treatment protocol to choose?"

I want to take some time with this answer. All of us who do psychotherapy already know that anxiety and depression are the most common complaints people bring to therapy. We spend time studying how to treat them, but there is no single place to get a manual for treating comorbid disorders. My intent with this book is to help you figure out where to start and where you might go as you progress with clients who present with co-occurring anxiety and depression. Let's examine the treatment protocol issue.

Due to the incredible rates of comorbidity, it seems prudent to operate as if these two disorders are facets of the same underlying neurochemical or brain-function problem. But it is the complex interplay of nature, nurture, and life experience that leads people to have different symptoms. Similarly, the course of treatment relies on the interplay among the client's history, response to interventions, and impact of symptoms on the course of treatment. The art of therapy lies in the therapist's ability to move with the client.

Despite the trend in the U.S. toward treating first with medication, psychotherapy is where clients with comorbid depression and anxiety belong. Although pharmaceutical interventions may be beneficial during the initial stages of therapy when clients may suffer from low energy and poor concentration that affect therapy compliance, research studies repeatedly demonstrate that cognitive-behavioral therapies are superior in the long run to psychopharmacology (Siddique, Chung, Brown, & Miranda, 2012; Wiles et al., 2013). In fact, the efficacy of psychotherapy for most clients is so strong that the American Psychological Association recently began a campaign using both video and print ads to urge people with mental health issues to try psychotherapy as the first-line treatment.

The considerable overlap between anxiety and depression suggests that we would do well to regard these disorders as one syndrome and treat it using a symptom-management approach. Farchione and colleagues (2012) argued effectively for what she called a "transdiagnostic approach" to treatment, noting that most manuals offer treatment approaches focused on one diagnosis, which forces clinicians to treat one disorder at a time. Farchione's research supports the effectiveness of inclusive styles of therapy such as cognitive restructuring, identifying and changing ineffective behaviors or maladaptive coping strategies, preventing avoidance, and exposure with response prevention. Various additional models of therapy, such as cognitive therapy, acceptance and commitment therapy (which uses mindfulness-based treatment), and exposure therapies lead the list of approaches to the symptoms.

Transdiagnostic treatment has been around for many years and has been known by different names, such as "multimodal" and "eclectic" therapy. This pragmatic approach to psychotherapy not only has been acknowledged as commonly practiced but also has been supported as valid (Lazarus, 1981; Palmer & Woolfe, 2000). For example, interventions for panic disorder have grown over the years to include a combination of psychoeducation, diaphragmatic breathing, and progressive muscle relaxation to decrease the probability of panic attacks occurring, along with cognitive interventions to change catastrophic interpretations of physical sensations and the meaning ascribed to the sensations. Other methods include interoceptive exposure to feared bodily sensations (e.g., dizziness, rapid heart rate) through spinning or exercise, and exposure to places that the individual has avoided for fear of having a panic attack. A similar set of treatment models is utilized for social anxiety.

Cognitive-behavioral therapy (CBT) works well when applied to symptoms of anxiety or depression, as it does not identify an underlying cause before treatment ensues. The broad range of CBT methods typically includes self-monitoring of depression or anxiety-provoking cues to identify and change maladaptive responses to them, metacognitive therapy to change thinking about symptoms, lifestyle changes, and identifying and correcting cognitive errors. CBT is widely recognized as effective for all age groups.

What about the underlying causes? When do you treat those? In my experience, effective symptom management is the key to subsequently identifying the underlying psychological causes that might drive these disorders. Those root causes can then be treated with appropriate psychotherapies. For example, with symptoms under control, a person who became anxious as a consequence of childhood experiences with an addicted parent can continue therapy to address that history and develop better ways of dealing with experiences that cause the depression or anxiety to reemerge.

In this book I will explain why anxiety disorders and depression are so often seen together. I will describe the brain structure and function that underlie comorbidity and discuss the hallmarks of each disorder. I will look at ideas for treatment protocols in the different presentations of co-occurring anxiety and depression. As always, in referring to clients throughout the book, confidentiality rules: All are amalgams of several people and do not describe any one individual.

ANXIETY +
DEPRESSION

CHAPTER I

WHERE TO START?

THE SIMILARITY between symptoms of anxiety and depression presents a serious clinical challenge. The case of Mary Jane was a classic example.

> Mary Jane persistently worried about the recurrence of her cancer, despite getting good reports from her physician. She felt like worry was ruining her life. It kept her awake at night, and it drove her to overschedule her days, with constant participation in community and family affairs. But no matter how busy she was, she continued to experience a constant undertow of worry about dying, and no amount of reasoning would resolve it. She sought therapy to help her stop worrying and be able to enjoy all her activity.
>
> When I began asking about her history, however, a more complicated picture emerged. Mary Jane ruefully admitted that she had some anger problems: She got frustrated with people she saw as being "slow" or "dense" and she had trouble not showing that she was irritated, which she constantly seemed to be. She knew she yelled too much. Closer

questioning also revealed another side to her activity level. Mary Jane laughingly stated that if she stopped moving, she would never start again, and that would be a disaster because she was the only one in her family who really got things done. Yes, her husband was employed, but that was where his contributions ended. She needed to supplement their income with her job and she was the one who drove the children to school and appointments, cleaned the house, and planned family events from birthday parties to vacations. She then joked that it might be easier to just give up trying to be happy altogether.

These revelations, offered in a lighthearted tone, were serious indications of the depression that was at the heart of Mary Jane's ruminating about dying. Her belief that worry was preventing her happiness was probably correct but not complete. She was feeling neither joy nor interest in life. She was busy due to obligations and her well-defined sense of duty, but she seemed more to be warding off hopelessness than seeking delight.

To me, Mary Jane's diagnostic picture was clouded by the presence of both anxiety and depressive symptoms: She was a busy worrier who was mostly depressed. Treatment for her would have to address both as well.

Mary Jane's case is a good example of how anxiety and depression can overlap. It is likely, in fact, that the high rate of co-occurrence is partly due to overlapping symptoms (Zbozinek et al., 2012). For example, people who endorse worry on a survey or in an interview also endorse the ruminative quality of depressive thinking. Examples of overlapping symptomatology include:

- Preoccupation or worry (topics vary—in depression, rumination is more likely about hopelessness or helplessness; in anxiety it is more apprehensive)

- Physical agitation
- Fatigue
- Sleep problems
- Irritability
- Loss of pleasure (notable as symptom of depression, but also prevalent in generalized anxiety disorder)

It is also well known that these disorders affect each other in reciprocal fashion:

- Anxiety precedes depression most often, as the weight of anxiety is depressing, but there is probably also a neuro-chemical reason for anxiety to come first, rooted in the impact of stress, which is a hallmark cause of anxiety.
- Suffering a panic attack while seriously depressed can lead to impulsive, ill-considered attempts to end life due to the press of terrifying feelings at a time when one is not feeling optimistic and resourceful. People suffering panic tend toward catastrophic explanations of life events and as a result their emotional regulation suffers. When they are also depressed, they do not readily see a way out of their suffering.
- People with social anxiety disorder tend to be passive, low on the scale of enthusiasm and energy, and are often shy and withdrawn. They are not necessarily depressed initially, but their isolation contributes to developing depression. In addition, their innate feeling of being socially incompetent and their lack of involvement in social activities make it tough to shake off depression when it occurs. Once depressed, they are less likely to push themselves toward more social experiences.

DISTINGUISHING BETWEEN ANXIETY AND DEPRESSION

Although the symptoms of anxiety and depression can be similar, there are certain features that can help a clinician decide which problem may be dominant. Table 1.1 shows what I listen for in an interview when I'm trying to parse the two.

TABLE 1.1 Side-by-side comparison of anxiety and depression symptoms.

ANXIETY	DEPRESSION
Worry is relieved by resolving the particular situation, but anxiety returns after a brief relief.	Worry is more like constant fretting over themes of worthlessness and inadequacy—static conditions that do not change.
Attitude is positive but includes "if only" thinking about what would resolve the problem once and for all.	Attitude is negative, and typically has hopeless or helpless themes that the problem cannot be resolved.
Energy may be high or low depending on the type of anxiety. Social anxiety often includes passivity and low energy; panic and generalized anxiety often involve high energy.	Energy is usually low, except in the highly active person who is becoming burned out. Then depression will emerge even if it did not preexist the burnout.
Sense of personal control may be excellent with generalized anxiety disorder clients, but external locus of control is common with panic and social anxiety.	While in a state of depression even people who have an internal locus of control feel unable to exercise it due to feelings of inadequacy and worthlessness.
Irritability is not constant. It results from tension and small things may cause behavior eruptions.	Irritability is persistent—like the person's temperament is sour.
Attention is disrupted by preoccupation with worries.	Attention is disrupted by low mental energy to hold focus.

Negativity isn't constant—it comes and goes with the perception of threat of danger (problems, losses, rejections, etc.). Life is not seen as being bad, but one's experiences are.	Negativity is persistent. Life is not seen as being good or as likely to work out well. People may see others, but not themselves, as having a good life.
Persistent high anxiety can overwhelm coping skills, leading people to be preoccupied with a "sick to the stomach" feeling, and to begin making mistakes in work and home life. This condition leads to depression, which might appear to be primary.	A depressed person with high anxiety will feel overwhelmed and have trouble functioning in work and home life. The anxiety might not be diagnosed as the problem when depression is evident, but it will hinder recovery.
Performance at work is often high but anxiety is experienced at home.	Signs of impairment often show up at home before they do at work.
Sleep problems are typically restlessness and problems quieting the mind to fall asleep. Worry dreams make sleep less restorative.	Sleep problems tend to be early-morning awakening or not feeling restored despite sleeping enough hours.

ASSESSING ANXIETY AND DEPRESSION

In assessing where to start, I look first at three issues:

- Physical health
- Readiness to change
- Mental energy

Physical Health

Physical health is unquestionably the first thing to look at. I've found that it's most often an issue with extremely revved-up clients and with low-energy clients.

Revved-Up Clients

Revved-up clients have high energy and display physical agitation. They are jittery and tense. Their mental process is also fast and jumpy. Their words spill over each other in a way that makes you think they are trying to tell you two things at once. Their communication does not have the racing, flight-of-ideas quality you may hear in mania, but you will get a sense that they are rushing to get it all out fast so that you can get busy treating them.

I often refer to revved-up clients as having "TMA" (too much activity). They tend to have a busy lifestyle or a very busy mental life, and when anxiety crests, they may move from one activity to another as is seen in attention deficit disorder (ADD). For example, one woman told me how she would find herself stopping in the middle of writing a check so that she could phone her sister to ask a question and then change a load of laundry and, returning to the check, find the dollar amount half written. The distinguishing feature here is that the anxious person without ADD remembers what he or she was doing!

When treating revved-up clients, it is important to rule out physical causes other than neurochemistry (see Chapter 2). Ask about and consider medical evaluation for:

- USE OF STIMULANT MEDICATIONS. Many drugs (such as asthma medication) have side effects that raise levels of adrenalin and norepinephrine. Make sure clients are responding appropriately to medications with this profile.
- FEMALE HORMONE LEVELS. Women who have suffered premenstrual distress seem to be especially sensitive to normal shifts in levels of hormones. This can lead to an overreactive stress response and create anxiety or depression.

That same woman is likely to have trouble during other life hormonal transitions. During perimenopause, for example, she may resemble revved-up clients, describing a "jumping out of my skin" feeling of easy irritability and physical agitation. At menopause, more depression may ensue.

- CONSUMPTION OF CAFFEINATED BEVERAGES AND ALCOHOL. Caffeinated beverages, especially "energy" drinks, can produce symptoms that look like anxiety. Ironically, alcohol, which is more often thought of as a calming agent, can be another cause of overarousal. People who binge on alcohol may experience intense physical agitation the following day from the body's normal process of detoxifying.
- LACK OF SLEEP. Emotions and physical reactions can become unstable with fatigue, and whereas one person may be exhausted, another can become agitated. Lack of sleep may be caused by any number of physical problems, such as pain or sleep apnea, to name just a couple.

Low-Energy Clients

Low-energy clients slouch in the chair as they tell you with minimal verbiage about their issues. Slow talking or less talking and long thinking are often initial signs of low energy. (Of course, these behaviors may also indicate introversion or hesitance to share information, but when they are coupled with other signs of low energy, you can be reasonably sure you're dealing with a low-energy client.) These clients radiate lethargy and you may find working with them tiring. Even when they are quite pleasant, you may feel a sense of helplessness in effectively treating their symptoms.

Low-energy people can be real worriers. Their anxiety may in fact dominate over depression, but genuine lethargy is a typical indicator of depression. As one of my clients described, "It is only when my anxiety about being fired skyrockets that I have enough mental oomph to overcome my lack of energy to do the work."

There are several physical issues to consider here:

- SLEEP. Is your client getting adequate rest? Waking up refreshed? If the answers to either of those questions is no, then evaluation of sleep is in order. The American Academy of Sleep Medicine website (in the resource list) can be a good starting point for developing a list of questions about sleep habits and sleep environment. Often simple interventions, such as no "screen time" for an hour before sleep, no work email after dinner, or sleeping in a dark room without the television on can make a world of difference. But you may well need to request a sleep study for sleep apnea, even in children.
- HORMONES. Low testosterone, which can affect women as well as men, is a common cause of low energy (as well as low libido). The physician doing the physical evaluation should be knowledgeable about hormones and their effects on mood and energy. Many of my clients seek advice from physicians trained in integrative medicine or from naturopaths when they suspect problems stem from hormonal imbalances and deficits.
- MEDICATIONS. Many medications, especially psychopharmacological drugs, are culprits for low energy; the list is too long to include here. A physician must be consulted.
- LOW VITAMIN LEVELS. Vitamin D deficiency tends to present as fatigue or depression; vitamin B deficiency can look like anxiety. Other low vitamin levels may have an impact as well. This is an easy problem to fix. For a time,

WHERE TO START?   9

large doses of vitamins prescribed or administered by injection by a physician may be necessary, and subsequent daily vitamins may be added to the diet. Also be aware that aging clients are more likely than younger clients to have adequate nutrition but malabsorption of vitamins, so physical issues like their level of intrinsic factor should be investigated.

- ANOTHER ISSUE RELATED TO AGING IS THE IN-CREASING LIKELIHOOD OF DISEASE PROCESSES. Anemia, low blood pressure, heart disorders, and many other causes of low energy should be investigated. This reinforces the need for careful physical examinations of clients.

- HIDDEN ALLERGIES. This issue is often harder to spot. The reserves of the low-energy client may be depleted during times of year when airborne allergens are prevalent. Food allergies can also produce symptoms of fatigue. One interesting possible indicator of food allergy is craving for foods or eating one primary food. A client who had significant fatigue issues told me the only beverage she drank was milk, and she drank a lot of it—at least six glasses a day. It turned out she had a latent food allergy to dairy that contributed to her fatigue and general feeling of malaise.

- NUTRITION. Even without vitamin deficiencies or food allergies, nutrition is often an issue for clients. Are they getting the right nutrients to build healthy, energetic brains and bodies? Check out the Reading & Resources section for books on eating right if you do not have a working knowledge of general nutrition.

Readiness to Change

Your clients' readiness to make changes in their lives depends on several factors. They must not only want to change but also see the problem for what it is and have the skills to move forward. Clinicians can learn a lot from questioning clients about how they perceive their problem to affect them, how they understand its origins, and what they have already tried to make things better.

Motivational interviewing is a style of therapy that has operationalized the process of questioning to help identify the client's stage of readiness to change. It also identifies the needs of each stage to promote change. Many clinicians understand and use this style in a less structured, intuitive way, even if they have not studied it. (See the Reading & Resources for more information about this style of working.) It is a remarkably helpful style for working with people with addictions, especially if they are not currently motivated to change their addictive behaviors. It is also very helpful with anxiety and depression, when clients often clearly need skills but may need some groundwork on motivation first.

When it comes to anxiety and depression, most people are motivated to feel better, but not every client enters treatment of his or her own volition. Often family members urge these clients to seek help, especially if panic or social anxieties cause stress for the family, as might happen if clients are reluctant to drive or go out socially without a companion. We start our inquiry into the client's condition by asking some version of the question "Why now?" When we hear that clients are there because someone sent them to get "fixed," we need to ask this question somewhat differently. We want to find out who wants them to change and what others say about their symptoms. Then we need to look for any personal motivation the client has to make a change.

I see this motivation issue most often with young adults who are socially anxious. They get sent to therapy by parents who want them to do better in college or find a better job, but these young people do not share that motivation except in a general way. They may not view their anxiety as the problem yet, instead identifying the problem as being outside of themselves—the university's classes are too large, for example, or the job market is too tight.

I've also seen the issue come up when one partner in a relationship wants the other to be less anxious, less depressed, more confident, and so on. The situation is especially challenging when clients firmly believe their problems would not be an issue if some external circumstance would change. They think their anxiety or depression would disappear if their partner would earn more money, stop being so angry, be more helpful, stop nagging, and so on—or if they themselves could just get a better job, feel physically better, move to a better house or neighborhood, and the like. Most people will not put effort into psychotherapy if they believe the rest of the world causes their problems.

Clients who are ready for change show an understanding that some (or most) of their problems in life are caused by their anxiety or depression and it is up to them to change that, even if they have no idea how to begin. They have enough internal locus of control to know they must put forth effort if they are going to feel better. Therapy may well start with the goal of developing this understanding.

Once clients are clearly ready and motivated to change, they also need skills, and these are built slowly with clients for their specific needs, which run the gamut from relaxation and breathing to attitude adjustment to social skills. That is where the largest segment of anxiety and depression symptom management occurs. Skills training is preparation for action steps but continues to be woven into the taking-action phase of treatment in the manner of course corrections that address obstacles to recovery as they emerge in treatment.

Mental Energy

Mental energy is critical to where you start in treatment. Quite often anxious clients with little depression are best off when it comes to energy. Their minds are busy and they can use their "revved" state to make persistent efforts to defeat anxious worry. One of the most anxious women I ever worked with told me she worried 20 hours out of 24. She could not turn her mind off to sleep until exhaustion claimed her and she got a few hours of mental respite. When I explained to her that she could use that persistence to do Thought-Stopping (see Chapter 9), she became relentless in interrupting negativity and made rapid progress.

The most severe problems occur when clients are low on energy—when the depressed symptomatology wins out. Therapy then has to focus on making very small steps that will raise energy enough to tackle the harder symptoms. For example, one male client in his forties came to treatment fairly motivated to feel better, but he spent most of his non-working hours sleeping or lying on the couch watching television. He often felt frantically anxious about whether he could maintain his employment with his poor attitude and he was becoming more isolated from his family than he had ever been. He knew he was gaining weight from eating fast food and getting no exercise, but every day he succumbed to one more pizza. Because this client had no mental energy to be persistent, we couldn't start managing anxiety with cognitive strategies. Instead, raising energy became the first goal of treatment.

Assessment Scales

Although many psychological measures require a psychologist to administer and interpret them, there are well-established clinical measures of anxiety and depression that can be used by any mental health professional. If your work requires outcome measures, these kinds of measures will be especially helpful. Some of these are:

- Beck Depression and Anxiety Scales
- Hamilton Depression and Anxiety Scales
- Anxiety Sensitivity Index (ASI)
- Children's Depression Index (CDI)
- Revised Children's Manifest Anxiety Scale (RC-MAS)
- Positive and Negative Affect Schedule (PANAS)—a 20-item self-report measure of positive and negative affect that helps differentiate anxiety from depression
- PANAS-C—a version of the previous scale for children, which also comes with a parent-report version
- Screen for Child Anxiety Related Emotional Disorders (SCARED)—a screening tool that has both a parent and child report
- Preschool Age Psychiatric Assessment (PAPA)—a parent interview to assess toddlers age 2 to 5 (this tool requires training to administer)
- Autism Diagnostic Observation Schedule, Second Edition (ADOS-2)—a semi-structured interview useful especially for previously undiagnosed adults with serious mental illness

These scales (and many others) not only can give you a quick sense of the severity of the depression and anxiety but also are a way to check on progress as they can be repeated at frequent intervals.

In the absence of these measures, you can follow a line of questioning based on *DSM-V* criteria for depression and anxiety to get a glimpse of what conditions are present. This won't help you with outcome measures, but it will help your diagnostic process for insurance billing and treatment-planning purposes.

ANXIETY AND DEPRESSION TYPOLOGY

The bigger question is deciding where to begin therapy when you have a mix of symptoms. When people have co-morbid disorders, they usually show up with a few common presentations of both disorders. In the world of official diagnoses, there are no diagnostic categories such as these; my hope is that the typology I outline in this book will provide you with a convenient way to identify the dominant symptoms and think about how treatment will develop. (See Figure 1.1 for a schematic of these typologies along the anxiety/depression spectrum.) When I am selecting treatment techniques for symptom management, I find it helpful to think about how my clients display dominant symptoms when they have both anxiety and depression. Although some clients require longer-term treatment, and I will make a few comments about how

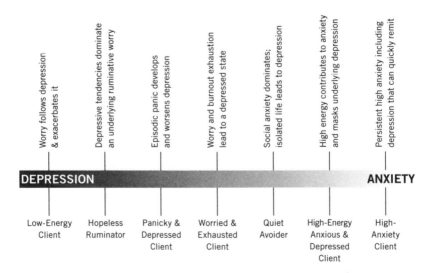

that might look, my focus is on shorter-term treatment to bring symptoms under control. The following seven client categories are my invention, based on years of clinical experience treating these problems.

THE LOW-ENERGY CLIENT. This client is easily identified as depressed because the mental and emotional tone is slow, concentration is impaired, and the client has little hope in his or her ability to do better. When this client is anxious and depressed, treatment focuses first on addressing the low energy. Often these clients start out with depression and anxiety arises as life failures occur.

THE HOPELESS RUMINATOR. This client may start out depressed and become anxious, or start out anxious and become depressed over time. The worries this person suffers are impervious to reason: The person feels hopeless about his or her life's changing for the better. Initial treatment in this case focuses on the client's negativity.

THE PANICKY & DEPRESSED CLIENT. When clients with depression— even mild or moderate depression— develop panic, their depression worsens. People with panic feel out of control, and when panic strikes, they feel terror. This is a hard emotional state from which to recover if they are depressed. Without depression, people feel okay when they are not panicking. When depression is present, it makes the between-panic state especially discouraging, and clients have less relief and less courage to face the panic. Learning to stop panic attacks before they occur and to limit their intensity if they occur is the first aspect of treatment, and this can be done effectively even when clients are depressed.

THE WORRIED & EXHAUSTED CLIENT. This is usually a client who is getting burned out. Whether depression is fueling the exhaustion or exhaustion is fueling the depression, there is no getting around the need to tackle lifestyle, stress management, and attitudes about personal responsibility at the outset of treatment.

THE QUIET AVOIDER. These clients almost always have social anxiety and depression. They hold back from life and do not feel much joy naturally due to their temperament and neurochemistry. As they continue to avoid, they miss opportunities to develop their talents and abilities, which leads to feelings of inadequacy and worthlessness that deepen the depression. Treatment starts with identifying clients' genuine motivation to interact more with others and moves quickly to building missing skills necessary to achieve their goals.

THE HIGH-ENERGY ANXIOUS & DEPRESSED CLIENT. This presentation of co-occurring anxiety and depression is more common when the client started out with generalized anxiety and tried using high activity to defeat it. When that inevitably fails to provide relief, the person starts to think he or she cannot stand life with this level of acute anxiety. Depression sets in when these clients cannot control the life situations they believe are causing their anxiety—as their efforts to control fail, they start to feel inadequate and powerless. For these clients, finding ways to reduce the high activity, be less perfectionist, and focus on meeting their own needs before taking care of others will provide mental and physical relief that lightens depression and anxiety.

THE HIGH-ANXIETY CLIENT. These clients are often higher in energy and suffer tremendously from a sense of physical agitation. The sick feeling in their gut that something is really wrong causes all manner of worrying to occur. This barrage of feeling is stressful and can lead to depression, as the client believes he or she won't ever feel better.

A FEW ASSESSMENT CAVEATS

It is important to note that the typology I offer in this book pertains to clients who can manage their symptoms and their lives with outpatient work. Clients who are suicidal or who display evidence of bipolar disorder require different types of interventions, including medication and hospitalization. Some clients have depression or anxiety symptoms so severe as to require hospitalization or intensive outpatient care. There are a few things to look for when assessing severity of symptoms. One is an inability to sleep resulting in fatigue that interferes with cognitive functions. Clients may tell you they not only are fatigued but also get confused or lose concentration. Another is a failure to fulfill requirements for work (whether keeping a house, caring for family members, or working outside the home). You should also look for evidence that clients are losing control of behavior too readily, such as inappropriately yelling or crying, especially when this loss of control interferes with clients' relationships with colleagues, bosses, or social acquaintances. These clients may fit the criteria discussed in this book after participating in more intensive initial treatment.

Another issue to consider is what kind of credibility you have with the client. Your clients' belief that you can help is paramount to getting them to participate. Therefore, the time you spend during assessment really *hearing* them may help them believe you know what they are going through. Do not be afraid to be an "expert" in their eyes in the beginning of treatment. Clients need to know that you know what you are doing.

Similarly, what kind of credibility does the treatment method have with the client? Has the client tried counseling before, and with what result? A major reason clients drop out of treatment is because they don't see how it could possibly work. Judicious use of psychoeducation may be your ally in this case. Learning why therapy methods will be effective encourages clients to trust, and any method works better if people trust it will work.

Unremitting anxiety also poses a challenge to treatment. Severe, persistent anxiety symptoms may require medication for the client to be able to focus on treatment and slow down his or her thinking enough to pay attention and focus on recovery goals.

A final issue to watch out for is isolation. While doing your evaluation, investigate alcohol use, online shopping, Internet pornography, and any addiction that may thrive in isolation. An isolated client may have developed addiction in an attempt to soothe the pain of isolation, but often connections with others are lost in service of the addiction. Also, isolated clients often struggle in treatment due to lack of external social support. Can you reconnect these clients with their prior social supports? Consider the value of also connecting them with self-help groups of any kind (addiction, grief support, divorce support, social-skills training, etc.). Most clients do better in treatment when they are connected to others who will support and encourage them in their goals for mental and physical health.

COURSE AND DURATION OF TREATMENT

Once you can identify what type of client you are treating, you have to make decisions about what kinds of methods to employ first. Chapters 3 through 9 each describe a typical case of the types of co-occurring anxiety and depression I mentioned earlier. I will discuss where therapy begins and what the treatment progress will be like. Again, this book does not address treatment of extremely severe symptoms—I am discussing cases in which clients can be seen on a weekly basis until their progress is better served by less frequent meetings. Although I am clearly a proponent of treating symptoms and seeing improvement in managing anxiety and depression, I want to clearly state that co-occurring anxiety and depression lengthen the process. When you move to treat under-lying causes in order to provide long-lasting relief and less chance of recurrence, the length of treatment will depend entirely on the clients' individual histories.

CHAPTER 2

UNDERLYING CAUSES

Neurobiology studies increasingly recognize that anxiety disorders reflect dysfunction in several systems of the brain. The relationship of these symptoms to underlying neurobiological causes is being better understood but there are still many unanswered questions. However, some basic knowledge of brain structure and function can help in understanding the basis for comorbidity.

THE ROLE OF BRAIN STRUCTURE AND FUNCTION

The development of depression and anxiety has to do with the interaction between a person's genetics and life history. It may be that "points of vulnerability" in the brain—due to genetics, disease, injury, or developmental insult—predispose certain people to depression or anxiety. If you have the genetic setup for it, you may develop depression or anxiety when life brings challenges.

Furthermore, the symptom profile may differ depending on the life circumstances one has encountered. For example, according to researcher Richard Shelton, it is "likely that the core pathophysiology of depression associated with early life adversity is different from non-trauma related disorders" (2007, p. 2). Similarly, different causes also result in different clusters of symptoms of anxiety. Temperamental factors clearly play a role in whether a person develops social anxiety or generalized anxiety, and biology affects panic attacks in direct ways. Considering the high rates of comorbidity between anxiety and depression, you would expect some commonality in the underlying causes of these disorders. In fact, family studies of heritability point to common genetic links. Yet although research using twin, sibling, and family studies shows a heritability of 30 to 40% for depression (and similar heritability for anxiety) the exact genetic links are not yet defined (Munago, 2012).

Neurotransmitters

The same problem exists in identifying exactly what role neurochemicals play in the development of anxiety and depression. That said, research suggests a few possible connections between neurotransmitters and anxiety and depression:

- Without sufficient serotonin, the brain seems more biased toward negative appraisal and pessimism. Many other consequences of low serotonin levels have been identified, such as poor impulse control, sleep irregularities, and inflexibility in problem-solving, among others.
- Low dopamine levels are implicated in loss of pleasure and reward as well as in insufficient attention. Many peo-

ple with depression suffer loss of pleasure and interest. Loss of pleasure is relevant to social anxiety as well, as socially anxious individuals do not reap great pleasure from social experiences that please most people without anxiety.

- Norepinephrine is a culprit in high arousal, agitation, and stress, causing tension and high blood pressure and initiating sympathetic-nervous-system activity. Severe imbalances of norepinephrine are associated with more panic attacks and more stressful stress.

- The excitatory neurotransmitters glutamate and acetylcholine are connected to feelings of agitation and sensitivity to environmental stimuli. When these are out of balance with GABA, people experience more of the mental and physical agitation of anxiety and depression.

- When transmission of GABA, an inhibitory neurotransmitter, is weak, responses are too strong or prolonged. People low on GABA may have panic attacks or worry unremittingly.

Brain Structure

Neurotransmitters do not tell the whole brain story, however—structures play a role, too. Without going into this in great depth, I'll offer a few examples:

- Weak connections between the anterior cingulate cortex and the amygdala result in stronger anxiety sensations and worry.
- Likewise, insufficient connections between the prefron-

tal cortex and the amygdala mean less restraint of fearful responses.

- An enlarged amygdala will result in greater perception of threat, leading to more fear of social rejection or more negative interpretations of life experiences.
- When the anterior cingulate cortex is not well connected to the cortex or to the amygdala and is low on serotonin:
  - behavior is inflexible,
  - cooperation suffers (children especially appear oppositional when anxious or depressed), and
  - the prefrontal cortex has trouble getting a calming message passed along to the overactive amygdala and arousal stays high.

How Do Function and Structure Interact?

The stress response is an example of structure and neurotransmitter function interacting to cause an entire system in the body to react. When the amygdala is overreactive to threat and negativity, it signals the stress response. If norepinephrine levels are dysregulated, too much stress response is initiated. Then, the agitated physical feelings that accompany the stress response convince the learning and remembering parts of the brain that the situation was really alarming. The new learning—"This was scary!"—occurs, causing an overreaction the next time that threat is perceived.

Let's review some of what we know about how brain structure and function underlie anxiety and depression. Table 2.1 sums up this comparison.

TABLE 2.1 **Brain structure and function in depression and anxiety.**

BRAIN STRUCTURE OR FUNCTION	ANXIETY	DEPRESSION
Amygdala: May be enlarged or undersupplied with serotonin, leading to preference for negativity and seeing more threat.	Overreactivity to possible risk (life seems threatening, people may be rejecting) contributes to panic and social anxiety.	Preference for negativity enhances the depressed mood and overwhelms brain's capacity to manage negative mood.
Stress Response System: Hypothalamus-pituitary-adrenal axis releases adrenalin and cortisol for energy and fuel for physical responses to stress. Chronic stress leads to serious impairments in immune and endocrine systems and affects brain function through depletion of the neurochemicals serotonin, norepinephrine, and dopamine and through damage from cortisol. Adrenalin raises physical tension and magnifies the arousal of norepinephrine. Stress also raises inflammation, a factor in depression.	Perception of threat and fear leads to overactive stress response, so stress feels worse and is harder on the body. Early life adversity makes small stress feel large as the brain reacts too strongly. Chronic stress depletes ability to function mentally and physically. Anxiety results from the overarousal of brain and body: States of tension and worry result, as well as increased likelihood of panic attacks. Loss of neurochemicals increases worry and decreases flexible problem-solving.	Early life adversity makes small stress feel large as the brain reacts too strongly. Chronic stress depletes ability to function mentally and physically. The depletion of serotonin contributes to increased negativity and overreaction to possible failure. This increases stress as feelings of loss of control cause stress for the client. Unable to mitigate stress, people feel lower self-esteem and exhaustion, leading to lower energy and fewer attempts to dispel stress. Inflammation raised by stress can contribute to depression symptoms.

Anterior Cingulate Cortex: With low supply of serotonin or with weak connecting fibers to and from the prefrontal cortex and amygdala, this part of the brain does not effectively conduct messages between emotion and thinking.	Suppression of fear signals is affected, so fear becomes stronger. Rigidity of thinking makes solving problems harder and anxiety increases. When anxiety rises, oppositionality can occur. As anxiety feels worse, avoidance of anxiety increases, leading to social anxiety and panic disorder.	Depression has strong cognitive components and a hallmark is the inability to see better solutions to life's challenges. Dysfunction in this area of the brain leads to rigid thinking and poor problem-solving, enhancing the depressed belief that things cannot change for the better.
Prefrontal Cortex (PFC): Different areas of this structure provide most of the functions we refer to when we talk about thinking. Analyzing information, integrating it with other information, making decisions and sticking to them, and creating meaning and stories about experiences are all functions of this area of the brain. Verbal and nonverbal problem-solving are conducted here.	When low on serotonin, the PFC does not have enough energy to push back against negativity from the limbic system (amygdala, hippocampus). Lacking skills due to too little exposure to new experiences, this part of the brain is missing mitigating information that would make new experiences less frightening. Thus, avoidance is increased due to fear of unknown situations.	Narratives are created in the PFC and people learn negative interpretations about self and others that get repeated by the PFC. Consequently, depressed attitudes about self, others, and the world are used to interpret new experiences in a less positive light. Depression becomes self-reinforcing. Low on serotonin, the PFC does not have enough energy to push back against negativity.

BRAIN STRUCTURE OR FUNCTION	ANXIETY	DEPRESSION
Basal Ganglia: These structures have several important functions in emotional life. They connect emotion and movement, they include the structures that register and anticipate reward, and they set the energetic tone for the brain. When GABA does not function efficiently, higher tension, tendency to panic, and excessive rumination occur. Low dopamine or poor reception of dopamine in this area of the brain lowers reward and anticipation of reward.	Panic attacks are often triggered by dysfunction in the basal ganglia. The basal ganglia may be implicated in excessive peripheral-nervous-system arousal that results in visible signs of social anxiety: blushing, sweating, shaking. High tension, high energy, and physical nervousness may also emerge. People with social anxiety have low reward from social experience and are less motivated to change their social habits than others may be.	Lack of reward leads to feelings of passivity, loss of interest, and little joy in everyday life experiences. Even bigger experiences are not anticipated with the same degree of pleasure. Loss of interest and no pleasure are both major indicators of depression.
Insula (and its connectivity to PFC): This part registers the somatic experience, noting how all of the body reacts and sensing what might be called the "affective" experience of a situation. Connecting to the verbal brain may be inefficient or interfered with by trauma.	When people misinterpret sensations as anxiety, they are more prone to have negative reactions to an experience. The somatic experience described to the self as negative leads to anxiety when it is reexperienced.	When feelings in the body are not easily articulated, depression can ensue due to inability to process and resolve negative experience. This seems to be a structural issue involving connections between the insula and verbal areas of the brain.

Low Supplies of Nutrients: We need sufficient proteins, vitamins, and nutrients to build healthy brains.	Vitamin B deficiency is strongly linked to nervousness and anxiety. Missing Bs, especially folate, without enough protein can inhibit the brain's ability to make serotonin.	Vitamin D deficiency is linked to depression. Studies suggest that providing the brain with omega-3 fatty acids and SAMe will decrease depression by helping the brain build healthy brain cells.

Neural Networking

Before I describe the possible causes of depression and anxiety, it would be helpful to discuss one feature of how the brain stores and retrieve memories. When something triggers one memory, a network of similar memories is automatically activated. Aspects of the memory—the emotion and the details—connect to similar experiences. This is an efficient way to recall information. However, in mood or anxiety disorders, it accounts for the tendency to recall every similar frightening, anxiety-provoking, or negative experience once a person starts to think about one experience. This leads to avoidance of any possible reoccurrence of a previous event.

This is true of moods as well, because a mood can change an experience or influence what we anticipate will happen. Once a person gets into a bad mood or begins to anticipate negative outcomes, the whole network of "previous bad moods" (poor outcomes) may "light up," causing the person to reenter the memories of negative thoughts, negative expectations, negative outcomes and disappointments, and even negative behavior patterns that reinforce the mood. An overarching goal of therapy is to interrupt negative networking and deliberately shift into a positive network. The ability to make that shift is a natural outcome of many of the techniques described in this book. When a person learns how neural networking underlies negative expectations or moods, this knowledge boosts the person's energy to apply the techniques that will ultimately interrupt the self-reinforcing neural networking.

THE FOUR MAIN CAUSES OF ANXIETY AND DEPRESSION

In psychotherapy we are very interested in life history and the outcome of experiences on our clients' functioning. For example, why does one person who is in a car accident subsequently show no signs of disruption in emotional life but another develops panic attacks when back on the road? We can attempt to identify risk factors such as early childhood adversity (Elovainio et al., 2007), but the variables are so numerous that exact predictions are impossible. They surely include genetics and brain structure and function, but they also include learning about self-efficacy, explanatory styles, cognitive function, and other aspects of self-reflective exploration of experience.

Help in sorting this out is underway. The Research Domain Criteria (RDoC), a new initiative sponsored by the National Institute of Mental Health, builds on existing models of anxiety and depression by looking first at observable behavior and neurobiological measures rather than the existing diagnostic categorical systems. It has identified different brain-based domains in which to assess anxiety. This will allow for new information to be included in our developing understanding of these disorders. As more and more data become available, this will be a powerful model for understanding anxiety and mood disorders (Craske, 2012).

A Practical Look at Underlying Causes

After working as a psychotherapist for nearly 40 years, I have noted that there are different types of depression and they seem related to different causes. For example, people whose depression develops after experiencing a serious loss seem to have more severe symptoms when they had an early life history of loss or adversity. Depression that emerges subsequent to a period of chronic stress seems different from the symptoms I've seen in people who described feeling depression most of their lives. I now think of these different types of depression as falling into clusters of symptoms based on the possible etiology of the depression.

The same sort of clustering effect occurs with anxiety disorders. I see people who have described themselves as worried from the day they were born, or as always sensitive and avoiding new experiences or people. But others tell me that a specific period of time or incident brought on anxiety that is now chronic.

The following ideas derive from my years of experience with clients and serve me in my thinking about causation as a general guideline. I see the types of depression and anxiety and their common underlying causes clustered in the following way:

- *Endogenous depression or anxiety* is genetic and neurobiological—the kind of condition people are "born to have."
- *Depression and anxiety as a consequence of early abuse or attachment problems* might look similar to endogenous depression and anxiety in the length of time symptoms have been around, but they are actually consequent to an early life loss, early life adversity, or failure of parents to provide a secure base and safe haven for the developing child.
- *Situational or stress-induced depression and anxiety* result when serious stress, often chronic, depletes the brain of

necessary neurotransmitters and consequently oversensi-
tizes it to stress.

- *Posttraumatic-stress depression and anxiety* seem to be the
outcome of traumatic experiences occurring later than
childhood. For example, depression, worry, panic, or avoidance may emerge after an accident, injury, natural disaster,
medical trauma, or combat-related trauma.

Let's look at each of these a little more closely.

Endogenous Depression and Anxiety
(The Brain You Were Born With)

Some people tell me they have been anxious or depressed all their
lives. They cannot remember a time when they were free of the
symptoms. When depressed, these people complain of low cognitive energy: "I just can't think about that now." "I just can't decide
what I should do." "I just sit and look at the work." They have persistently negative mood, irritability, and limited pleasure or interest
in daily life. They suffer from a tendency to be passive and hard
to motivate—their attitude toward therapy can be summed up as
"what's the use?" When no particular trauma or stress seems to
be causing this lethargy, endogenous depression is the most likely
culprit.

I see endogenous anxiety most often in socially anxious people, who, like those with depression, tend toward passivity. Most
socially anxious people not only are passive but also take little
delight in the kinds of social encounters that are intrinsically pleasurable and motivating for people without the neurobiological setup
for this kind of anxiety. Some people are also neurobiologically
prone to having panic attacks, and at some point in life they have an
attack so alarming that they begin to fear having another, triggering

full-blown panic disorder. Endogenous anxiety is also revealed in the person who says, "I have always been a worrier," and who talks about worrying as part of his or her identity. Sometimes these people are also high-energy, and when anxiety intensifies, they seem driven. That energy level is obviously different than the lethargic quality of depression, but in both situations, the condition has been there throughout much of life.

One hypothesis about the cause of this set of symptoms is a genetically determined inadequate supply of neurotransmitters, such as serotonin, norepinephrine, dopamine, acetylcholine, glutamate, and GABA, all of which have effects on mood and energy.

- Low levels of serotonin result in negativity, a tendency to ruminate, and less mental energy. Serotonin is also a contributor to the sense of satisfaction when effort is exerted to achieve something. Lack of serotonin can make it harder to see positive outcomes.
- In the right amounts, norepinephrine gives an overall state of arousal necessary to feel both physical and mental energy. When it is insufficient, underarousal or lethargy results. Too much norepinephrine creates high energy that can easily tip into tension and vigilance.
- Dopamine is necessary to feel focused and also to feel reward. It directly helps people to learn that what they just experienced was pleasurable and thus provides the motivation to "do that again!" Loss of pleasure or interest is a feature of both social anxiety and depression.
- Low levels of the activating neurochemicals glutamate and acetylcholine can sometimes be a problem, but more often levels of these chemicals are too high, resulting in agitation and leading to sensations of anxiety that fuel worry, ten-

sion, and anxiety sensitivity. They also affect new learning and adapting—the goals of therapeutic interventions.

- GABA is necessary to slow the brain's activity and is most implicated in chronic worry with generalized anxiety and in panic attacks.

Depression and Anxiety as a Consequence of Early Abuse or Attachment Problems

Among the most challenging symptoms of depression, panic, and generalized anxiety that I have observed are in people with a history of childhood neglect or abuse or who had insecure or anxious attachments to parents or caretakers. People with a history of abuse may feel acutely anxious both physically and mentally. The high agitation of acute anxiety may be unremitting, and small stresses are felt in the body as "big deals." These people find it nearly impossible to turn off worry because they feel disturbed so much of the time.

They may also experience remarkable, dramatic shifts of mood from feeling okay to feeling seriously depressed. Such depression also manifests in a cognitive "default mode" of negative expectations about the world—no one is going to surprise this person with a positive outcome. People with this type of depression also appear unable to calm down or "self-soothe" during times of challenge. They tend to plunge into despair whenever minor upsets occur. When they plunge, they may engage in impulsive, self-injurious behavior: drinking, gambling, having risky sexual escapades, or even threatening or attempting suicide. If they suffer panic attacks, which might be an expectable consequence of adverse life experiences, they are at higher risk for impulsive and self-injurious acts.

When I observe a person plummeting from relative equanimity into abject misery and hopelessness, I look for an early life history of adversity that might explain this, because it will affect our treatment choices. Not only are these clients not expecting much of others, but their plunges into despair are like "falling off a cliff" and are very difficult to interrupt.

Another outcome of early life adversity is a state of chronic worry about what others are thinking and doing. A state of vigilance begins. It can include performance anxiety, in which people feel at risk whenever they might be scrutinized, which leads to an aversion to being the center of attention in any way and, eventually, to social anxiety. But the state of vigilance also leads to generalized anxiety and worry.

Depression and anxiety take on a particular quality when they stem from serious and repeated adversity very early in life, created by the very people who should have been caretakers. It is quite likely that early adverse events in life, particularly abuse but also repeated neglect, "contribute significantly to the potential for a depressive episode" (Kendler, Thornton, & Gardner, 2001, p. 585.) This risk is based in several potential outcomes of repeated adverse stress early in life:

THE STRESS RESPONSE AND ADVERSITY. One cause of this type of depression and anxiety is due to changes in the stress response (Bergmann, 1998), exaggerating the effect of small stresses due to a permanent overreactivity to stress.

- Cellular changes occur when a child does not receive comfort for distress. Over time, those changes result in diminished effectiveness of responses to new stressors (Kendler et al., 2001). This is observed to be a genetic predisposition coupled with a "dose-specific" impact of stress (Nemeroff, 2004; Shelton, 2007). It may play a role in inability to turn off stress, making tension, anxiety, and depression more likely.

- A distressed child who is not comforted becomes frantic and then shuts down (Schore, 2003). The neurobiological impact of repeated neglectful or traumatic failures to receive comfort is a shutdown at the level of the parasympathetic nervous system, creating a state of biological and psychological despair. This biological shutdown of sympathetic arousal has repercussions: The arousal will be shut down much faster when a similar arousal is felt at a later time. This makes it harder to create effective solutions to problems, because the shutdown is not only physical but also emotional and mental.

- Memories that are implicit—felt on a physical level without specific recall (Siegel & Hartzell, 2003)—result in fewer efforts to soothe oneself and contribute to negative expectations of the outcome of new experiences. Also, the unpredictable nature of parental responses can intensify chronic, acute anxiety and make for persistent vigilance to personal mistakes or to the responses of others around us.

- Exposure to this early life adversity increases the risk of depression and anxiety due to the changes in the neurobiological responses to stress and also in the coping style, which becomes maladaptive later in life (Felitti et al., 1998; Nemeroff, 2004). People who have suffered aversive early life experience tend to search for soothing in maladaptive behaviors that can become self-destructive, such as poor self-care, poor eating habits, smoking or other substance use, and high-risk sexual behaviors.

AVOIDING SOCIAL EXPERIENCES AFTER EARLY LIFE ADVERSITY. As the child matures into adolescence, the propensity to feel less reward and make less effort toward reward shows up in the tendency to make poor social connections and feel more depressed. Avoiding situations in which the adolescent feels uncertain leads to social concerns and generalized anxiety adds to the lack of pleasure in social experiences. By adulthood this person may easily be triggered to worry and have severe inability to use rational self-talk and self-soothing when facing trouble.

This is a likely outcome for a child who is repeatedly left when distressed without comfort by caregivers. That child first becomes frantic and then resigned and hopeless, in effect shutting down emotionally. Repeated experience of this kind of neglectful or even traumatic attachment failure can result in constant acute anxiety and in an adult mental default mode of hopelessness and low expectations of self and others, which cause self-reinforcing plunges into psychological despair. Over the course of life, the way people habitually think about themselves develops into self-image. The self-image that emerges from implicit memory of despair is an intrinsic sense of worthlessness. The trigger to plunging into depression can be any situation, inner thought, or conversation that elicits fear of being disappointed, abandoned, or neglected.

Situational or Stress-Induced Anxiety and Depression

The natural outcome of prolonged stress is anxiety and depression. Chronic stress seems to be the most likely cause of simultaneously emerging depression and anxiety because of the many ways stress acts on physical, mental, and emotional states. The colloquial expression "burnout" sums up what happens in chronic stress (or situational anxiety and depression).

When people are exhausted by stress, pronounced physical lethargy and isolation emerge as people struggle to recuperate. Sleep disruption is one common outcome of stress, and people may isolate themselves to try to get rest or sleep. But isolation leads to depression. Attempts to relax with alcohol or over-the-counter medications may lead to additional problems with depression and even addiction. The symptoms are self-reinforcing because it is hard to challenge thoughts of sadness, discouragement, or meaninglessness when you remain exhausted and isolated. Situation-induced depressions may occur following serious personal loss (job, spouse, death of a loved one), work burnout, or long-term care of a sick family member.

The problem with situational depression and anxiety is that fixing it requires not only attitude adjustment but also a situation adjustment. Many times people face real-life challenges they can't avoid: the death of a spouse, the necessity of caring for a parent with Alzheimer's, long hours at work to keep a job. If the person is to fully recover, the circumstances must change. That said, one way to begin treatment is to change the way the person is handling the stressful situation mentally or behaviorally. Anxiety and depression make it hard, but the person may need to change thinking patterns about the stressor or change how the stress is dealt with behaviorally.

Once people are burned out, changing the circumstances or changing their behavior in the circumstance is exceptionally challenging. Cognitive rigidity (a failure to see options to do things differently), common to depression and generalized anxiety, sets in with burnout. For example, a person who is caring for a sick or disabled family member may feel locked into the pattern of caregiving and not take advantage of relief opportunities such as having a person or an agency outside the immediate family take over for a while. The caregiver may see only the obstacles and not the benefits in getting relief—for example, he or she may see the patient disturbed by an unfamiliar face and fear it will worsen the illness, but not recognize how his or her own tension and worry affect the quality of time with the patient.

Such mental rigidity may be evident in the hours a person puts in on the job or in repetitive, ineffective attempts to solve problems that could easily be resolved if the person had the energy to consider different solutions. The lack of resiliency in thinking and the desperate fatigue that envelops this kind of depression and anxiety are most striking.

In fact, the symptoms that result from chronic situational stress are the same kinds of symptoms present when you are sick: fatigue, loss of interest, loss of appetite, and so on. Those symptoms lead a person to rest, which is a great help in recovering from an infection or virus. Stress creates the same kind of changes in the brain that infection creates, but because there is no illness to recover from, the symptoms are those of depression. And they don't go away while the stress continues. The more a person tries to push through, the worse the impact of the stress on physiology.

Situational burnout can be seen in any line of work and at any age. Regardless of the specific circumstances, however, several issues may be at play:

GENETIC VULNERABILITY. A person may have some genetic or neurobiological vulnerability that is waiting for the right situation to express itself. Chronic stress at a nontraumatic level damages health in many ways and affects the brain by depleting neurochemistry. Under conditions of stress, the brain uses up available supplies of serotonin, norepinephrine, and dopamine. As those neurotransmitters are depleted, the typical depression symptoms of less mental energy, less interest in the world, loss of pleasure, and less physical energy become increasingly evident. Anxiety also comes into play as stress prepares the body for action and muscles get tense, norepinephrine rises, and worrying takes hold. Also symptomatic of both anxiety and depression is how rigid problem-solving becomes, with ruminative thinking together with the loss of mental clarity and low energy, preventing a creative look at solving the stressful situation.

ISOLATION. When stress is ongoing, people may try to escape it and "recharge" by isolating themselves from people and activities they previously enjoyed. However, isolation rarely succeeds in recharging the person, especially when the stress is chronic. Isolation from one's social life and friends may be an expectable outcome of devoting increasing energy to handle the stressful situation, but contact with social groups is a major salve to the wounds of stress (Eisenberger, Taylor, Gable, Hilmert, & Lieberman, 2007). Social connections have long been known to buffer stress and mitigate its damaging effect on physical and emotional health, and the connection between stress and consequent illness has been indisputably shown (Cohen et al., 2012).

When people participate with others in rewarding activities, the "I feel good" neurochemical dopamine flows, as do others such as oxytocin (a "soothing" neurotransmitter that is released when one is touched, befriended, or otherwise in pleasant contact with others). These neurochemicals make people feel soothed, calmer, and refreshed. In isolation one misses out on that positive reward. Isolation itself becomes a trigger for depression. People with a neurobiological setup for social anxiety are already low on dopamine and less involved with others, so when they get more isolative with stress, they are even more likely to become depressed as well as anxious. Research suggests that isolation leaves people not only feeling alone but also less able to cope; cognition is affected and it is harder for them to make good decisions (Eisenberger et al., 2007). "I can't" is hard for people with situational stress to say aloud, but they think it a lot. In contact with others, they will be able to gain access to help and be less overwhelmed.

Posttraumatic-Stress Depression and Anxiety

Posttraumatic stress disorder (PTSD) is another cause of depression and anxiety, as this disorder encompasses many psychological symptoms. After a traumatic experience, people may develop triggers or "cues" that their amygdala reads as warning of danger. Panic attacks can result when something in the environment cues the brain to panic as it did during the trauma. Over time, those cues generalize and panic attacks come on in response even to situations unrelated to the trauma. Consequently, the PTSD sufferer starts to avoid any possible place where panic might occur. Panic disorder becomes established, often rapidly, subsequent to trauma.

One particularly insidious impact of PTSD is the helplessness that can cause depression and make panic attacks much harder to cope with. (In fact, depression coupled with panic leads to higher risk of suicidality.) Helplessness is a feeling that is hard to ignore because it feels so believable—one feels helplessness physically, emotionally, and mentally. Helplessness gets in the way of motivation to try to improve a situation.

The impact of helplessness makes sense in a couple of ways. First, traumatic stress sensitizes memory so that recall of trauma is easily triggered. This is related to the impact of dopamine in combination with norepinephrine, both of which flood the brain during the experience of trauma, forming powerfully etched memory associations. In other words, the trauma is vividly learned and easily recalled after it is over. Second, neural networking makes this even more pronounced. Recalling the trauma causes one to enter the network of memory that holds all of the details—including physical sensations, all of the environmental stimuli, all of the thoughts, and all of the affect of that situation *and* other similar situations. In this way, helplessness is self-reinforcing.

The depression of PTSD can be moderate or very severe and even suicidal ideation can emerge. The severity of the depression depends on the pre-stress health and resilience of the person suffering the traumatic event. However, no matter what the overall severity of the depression is, it can manifest in sudden feelings of helplessness, which are set off by emotional or environmental events. Often people may not even recognize what triggered the helpless, depressed state.

Helplessness is a common feature of depression, but is remarkable in the person suffering PTSD. It is a cognitive as well as emotional feature, because in this type of depressed state a person feeling helpless is less likely to generate solutions to problems. Victims of trauma may even feel helpless about having depression, which may seem to them like a replay of the helplessness they experienced during the initial trauma. They have a hard time believing anybody can help them and have even less confidence that they will ever be able to help themselves.

Why does traumatic stress have such an impact on mental health? The majority of trauma victims never develop PTSD, but for those who do, even small subsequent stressors are mentally and physically experienced with disproportionate power. Rachel Yehuda has speculated that people who are vulnerable to developing PTSD may well have a risk factor of low cortisol, creating a problem in turning off stress even before the trauma occurs (Yehuda, 1997; Yehuda & LeDoux, 2007; Yehuda, Harvey, Buschbaum, Tischler, & Schmeidler, 2007).

However, we also know that trauma resets the brain's stress-response system to a more intense level, leaving in its wake a perpetually higher level of norepinephrine, which means more sensitivity to triggers for stress and more intense physical reactions (Bergmann,

1998). As stress becomes more stressful, the risk of anxiety and depression goes up.

Both factors may be at play—a person's genetic risk for depression or anxiety, and the effect of the trauma, changing a healthy, balanced brain to a less balanced and more vulnerable brain—making traumatic stress a major contributor to mental-health problems.

GETTING STARTED

In helping clients with co-occurring anxiety and depression, I have found that it is not necessary to treat one disorder or the other first, but rather to look at the combinations of anxiety and depression that seem most common and weave together symptom-management strategies that will foster energy and optimism for treatment while reducing symptoms.

CHAPTER 3

THE LOW-ENERGY CLIENT

THE LOW-ENERGY client is the closest to pure depression on the comorbid anxiety and depression spectrum. The following checklist indicates the main characteristics of low-energy clients.

||||||||||||||||||||||||||||||||||||||||||||||||||||||||||||||||||||

_____ *Lethargy.* The client may continue to work but complains of fatigue at small expenditures of energy and spends many nonworking hours napping, lying around, watching television, or otherwise doing very little.

_____ *Oversleeping.* Sleep may be excessive and nonrestorative.

_____ *Loss of interest.* The client does not have hobbies, and though the client might have had hobbies at one time, he or she often refutes this.

_____ *Lack of involvement with others* (though not necessarily isolation). The client may do required family activities or maintain minimal contact with friends, but he or she typically does very little and rarely initiates contact.

_____ *Failure to answer the phone or return messages.* Again, this speaks to a lack of involvement with others.

_____ *Overeating.* The client may be overweight, as eating is one of the few pleasures he or she experiences.

_____ *Rumination.* This is where anxiety will be present, usually as preoccupation with what will happen, what has gone wrong, what to do, and what cannot be changed.

There is no question—depression is the dominant symptom set of low-energy clients. Their demeanor is flat in every way: They sit quietly and talk without emphasis or much detail. They do not describe lives full of activity, and they complain of exhaustion, even from minor exertion. They may report having poor concentration or memory issues. You're also likely to hear about life losses and failures—even their story sounds like pure depression.

In many ways, these clients will present a picture of lifelong low energy or low drive even though they may be talented and function well in various parts of their lives. They seem to me the model of endogenous depression. Set up by neurobiology, they are primed to become depressed. Often they will tell you that they've always felt depressed and were able to manage it until some life circumstance made the situation worse, prompting them to seek treatment. I think these clients often do not know how depressed they are until it is moderate in severity, because they have little to contrast their inner experience with. Unlike people who once felt good and can recognize depression when it sets in, low-energy clients see their current state as just "more of the same." This lengthy history of depression complicates their treatment because their low expectations of life limit their view of how things could be. This affects their motivation, because they don't have a history of feeling excited or enthused about things. But despite their low expectations about the future, these clients often have a desire to feel better.

So, what would lead you to look for comorbid anxiety? I usually see the anxiety more clearly when it blocks the client from moving forward. Low-energy clients may feel anxious about a situation they do not have the energy to face, or about what life would be like if they had more energy. They may experience that potential of life without depression as anxiety-provoking because they do not have a self-image that incorporates energetically meeting life's demands, and they fear that they will fail to keep up with life if they lose the depression. For example, they may desire more social time but feel anxious about pursuing it because they have failed to maintain friendships in the past. It doesn't matter whether those "failures" were due to their depression: Failure deepens low self-worth and increases anxiety in a reciprocal fashion.

But comorbid anxiety in low-energy clients is secondary to depression and functions more like a drag on recovery than a very active symptom.

A CASE OF THE LOW-ENERGY CLIENT

John, age 52, came to see me at the urging of his primary physician, complaining of a sense of immobility and fear that he was going to fail at work if it got worse. When I asked about when he started feeling this way, he calmly said he had always been like this but it had gradually worsened over time. Although successfully

self-employed to date and interacting with his employees as neces-
sary and without conflict, John was participating only minimally
in family life at home. He also stated that he hadn't been sociable for
several years. He felt little motivation to do much, but he knew he
was disappointing his immediate family. His married son "didn't
need a lot" from him, but John rarely spent time with his grandchil-
dren. His wife, who also worked, was busy with her own life and
did not place many demands on him. They had no sex life anymore
but John said he didn't miss it.

ASSESSMENT

Of course you immediately wonder about physical health with the
presentation of low energy as marked as John's. I suspected that he
might have any of a number of issues and carefully asked about them.

Physical Health

The lethargy is the first and most prominent feature of health to
examine. There are significant potential physical causes of low
energy, and these must be medically screened for and treated appropriately. Therapy can progress best when medical attention is being
given to those situations requiring it.

For low-energy clients, assessment of physical health must
consider:

- SLEEP. In the absence of primary insomnia, sleep apnea
  would be a strong contender for awakening without feeling
  refreshed or for sleeping too much and still feeling tired.
  There are other parasomnias, such as restless legs, as well as
  less common disturbances in sleep architecture that might
  require a sleep study.

- VITAMIN LEVELS. Low vitamin D can be a culprit for fatigue and low energy, and in the U.S. it is becoming a common problem, especially among adults with little time outdoors. Although other nutritional features might play a role in energy, low vitamin D is not uncommon even in well-nourished people.

- LOW IRON OR ANEMIA. Another reason for a blood test! These imbalances may be major or minor, but for people who have not had a thorough physical, they must be considered as potential causes of low energy.

- HORMONES. For all adults, thyroid can be a significant cause of tiredness and sluggishness, and a full thyroid panel is necessary to see if the levels of thyroid hormone are not only sufficient but also being utilized well. In women, menopause can trigger depression with fatigue due to significant drops in estrogen, but this presentation of low energy (when caused by hormones) is more often connected to testosterone. When assessing a man over the age of 40, consider low testosterone as an underlying cause of low energy. Hormonal changes usually come on slowly, so people often do not realize something physical can be at the root of their low mental energy.

John slept way too much without feeling refreshed. I suspected sleep apnea, but I also wondered about vitamin D, thyroid, and testosterone levels. He sheepishly said that his physician had recommended a sleep study, and he was supposed to take vitamin D and testosterone but had not gotten around to doing that. Why? Low energy!

Readiness to Change

It takes a lot of energy to make an appointment and show up, so it is wise to inquire about the client's motivation to go to that trouble. When low-energy clients present themselves in a therapist's office, it is time to wonder who wants them to change and whether they not only recognize their problem but also feel prepared to feel or act differently. The willingness to change takes energy by itself, and that energy will be stronger if there are good reasons that are personally motivating.

- Positive motivation can be found when a client fears losing a love relationship.
- A physician might insist on therapy if he or she is going to continue to prescribe medications for depression or anxiety. Low-energy clients may want what they perceive as the "easy fix" for depressed mood—SSRI medication—and the physician may wisely convince them that there is more to the story and make a referral for psychotherapy.
- Positive motivators that produce readiness to change in low-energy clients are often work-related:
  - Sometimes it's fear of losing a job. This is something most people take pretty seriously and it can prompt motivation to make changes.
  - Self-esteem can take a big hit with job loss, and esteem issues can help people be genuinely ready to make a change.
  - At times the awareness of declining performance is a motivator in clients who are accustomed to reasonable productivity.

But those motivations do not always apply:

- The job issue could be one of not wanting the current job and not knowing how to quit.
- The compliance with the physician referral might be simply to keep the prescription with no real readiness to make a change. Alternately, a client may prefer to get off of medication or never start it, and may be in therapy to avoid medication and its side effects.
- If clients are pushed by a significant other to appear in therapy, they may have low personal motivation or even a desire to sabotage therapy. They may "fail" therapy to demonstrate their own power to choose (even though that might not be an entirely conscious decision).

The question is whether the client genuinely sees the need to make a change for his or her own wellbeing. Low-energy clients might want their significant other to be happier, but they may also resent being "forced" into therapy just so someone else is happy. Spending some time developing a mutually clear understanding of what they have to gain and how therapy can help can improve motivation and help clients get over the first hurdle of low energy: willingness to change.

> *John brought himself to therapy at the urging of his physician, and he indicated that he thought life would be better if he felt more energy. He also wanted to get off his medication. But in talking about what would be better if he felt more energy, he was clearly ambivalent about whether maintaining his marriage was a priority. He did not want to lose it, but he also had some unresolved anger at his wife. He did, however, have a real concern about work and*

feared that he would lose his clients if he got worse. He liked making money and knew he had to work for several more years before he could comfortably retire.

Mental Energy

This is obviously a factor in therapy with the low-energy client. Poor attention or loss of concentration can interfere with attempts to make change or even to utilize the therapy session itself. Assessing the amount of available energy may occur over several sessions as you gauge whether the client is thinking about or doing therapeutic assignments. Mostly the challenge is to make suggestions that require very small amounts of energy at the outset of therapy, assuming that you will be going slowly. One indicator that low-energy clients can do therapy successfully without medication is their ability to concentrate on work-related or household tasks long enough to complete them.

John seemed low on mental energy in our conversation, but he also described his work as requiring a lot of creativity. I speculated that he did have some mental energy but was using his supply of it at work. I would draw on that as we began the therapy process.

Burnout

One other major contributing factor to low energy can be the impact of chronic stress or burnout. People can get burned out and low on energy regardless of whether they are first depressed: Chronic stress drains mental, emotional, and physical reserves. When a person starts out with a mild or subclinical depression, the depression can worsen and look like low-energy depression. The lower the energy falls, the more the person tends to cut out positive activity like socializing or exercising. Jane was a good example of this.

> *Jane had probably always suffered from some depression. She had limited experience with romantic relationships but a wide circle of friends. When a recent job promotion placed significant demands on her, however, she began to suffer burnout, and she stopped socializing, felt blue, and gained weight, often eating alone and for most of the night as a way to put some pleasure into the end of her workday. Her presenting symptoms were similar to John's, but because the cause was chronic stress, therapy had to start with stress management and seeing if Jane could alter her situation to relieve the stress.*

THERAPEUTIC RELATIONSHIP

A big issue in beginning work with any client is the therapeutic relationship. I am typically directive with clients early in therapy for symptom management, and as we move along I become more collaborative, supportive, insight-oriented, and so on. As we all know, after extratherapeutic factors, the biggest agent of change for every client is the relationship with the therapist. We want to strike a balance between their belief that we know how to help and our respect for their wisdom about what is wrong and what to do about it.

As with every client, feeling heard is important for the low-energy client, but feeling *not judged* is critical. Often this client feels the weight of judgment simply due to our cultural bias toward being busy all the time. We do not live in a culture that values silence, reflection, quietness, or relaxation. So low-energy clients may start out, without even realizing it, feeling defensive or expecting to be judged just for their energy level and lack of high-drive achievements. Communicating your understanding and acceptance of where they are is more important with these clients than with any other of the anxiety-and-depression types. You cannot start to move them without their belief in your non-judgmental stance.

Another issue in relationship-building with low-energy clients is their feeling of being pushed when they don't have enough energy to perform. The therapy relationship must be more supportive at the outset and become collaborative faster than with higher-energy clients who thrive on direction and expectations. The collaboration improves motivation, as respect for these clients' pace of movement helps them feel more able to move.

Low-energy clients also need to be told that they are not unusual or alone in their complaint. Men in particular are sensitive to this, as other men do not usually own up to emotional pain. It is reassuring if you can tell these clients that others (men included) have had these problems with low-energy depression and anxiety and have been able to feel better.

Walking the line between being encouraging and having expectations can be a bit tricky, but it is the final piece in establishing a solid therapeutic relationship. Your confidence that some of your ideas can help them achieve their goals can boost their mental energy.

John felt bad about his low energy and was judging himself pretty harshly. He was also carefully assessing my attitude toward him, and he made several self-deprecating, sort of sarcastically amusing remarks that might have invited me to agree: "This is pretty bad for a guy who's supposed to be the boss, isn't it?" Although I am usually inclined to make humorous or ironic replies to this kind of statement, I thought it was better to stick with reflective listening until I knew him better and could appraise the meaning behind the humor and how sensitive he was to responses to it.

John was open to suggestions, but like most with low energy, he was not ready to take action. I told John what I tell every client: "I will make suggestions but it is entirely up to you whether you want to try the ideas or not. If they don't help enough, we can add something to the mix. And I will listen to your responses as we go to see how we can modify suggestions so they work best for you personally."

Again, however, it's important to remain keenly aware of whether your low-energy clients are interpreting your suggestions as pressure to make changes or as negative judgment. This was particularly true with Jane.

It didn't take long for me to see that Jane was very sensitive to expectations. I quickly backed off anything that sounded like a suggestion to do something right away, especially if it was not work-related. She was still stuck in her one solution of working more to relieve her workload. She would need some time to know I was not asking even more of her. We stayed on themes of understanding and support for several sessions, discussing how things in her life evolved to this point. That also served the purpose of identifying corrective measures she might be willing to undertake when she was ready.

ADDRESSING THE SYMPTOMS

An obvious place to start with every client is in making relevant lifestyle changes, such as improving nutrition or adding exercise. Research supports the idea that people make lifestyle changes slowly, and that they need to feel free to change the way they want to if the change is going to be successfully accomplished.

Lifestyle

The low-energy clients are most in need of starting to move physically if they are going to feel better. I believe that all of my clients are responsible for their own lives and I cannot make them do anything. What I can do is help them acquire information, skills, and self-awareness to make changes they desire for themselves. With low-energy clients, that is the perfect way to avoid the appearance of judging or pushing them too fast.

> *Once we were in agreement about what he eventually needed to do to improve his health, such as follow up with his physician regarding vitamins and testosterone, I did not ask John every session about whether he had scheduled an appointment. I asked him to inform me when he made appointments and then to inform me about their outcome. It took him months to arrange a sleep study and to start using the continuous positive airway pressure (CPAP) machine, but he finally did it. He also eventually started the vitamins and testosterone.*

How Much Will Lifestyle Changes Help?

The shift in energy may seem imperceptible at first—it's like starting a train rolling from a dead stop. Other clients with better energy may notice faster changes when they begin to exercise or sleep better, but low-energy clients are starting from a place of such inertia that it takes time to improve. Therapy can provide reasonable encouragement to stay with it.

> *For John, changes were minimal at first and he felt discouraged. After a few months, however, he noticed was that he finally had the energy to start walking a bit after dinner and to do a few weekend chores. He also started to watch his food intake, and his*

motivation began to increase when the scale showed that he'd lost a couple of pounds.

Specific Therapy Tools for Change

Lifestyle changes are essential for most low-energy clients, but they take time. Therapy can help get these clients moving by addressing the emotional, mental, and behavioral aspects of the client's disorder. There are several types of interventions to start with.

Prime the Pump and Get the Train Rolling

These two techniques work very well for low-energy clients. Priming the Pump is the first step. They start out with a task they are not getting done—often one that takes time to finish, such as mowing the lawn, putting groceries away, or repetitive work tasks such as filing. Clients then determine the largest amount of time they can commit to doing the task, or what they feel up to doing at the moment. The amount of time must be small enough that clients do not feel pushed beyond what their low amount of energy can handle—for example, they may decide that they can handle 10 minutes of mowing the lawn. After the 10 minutes of mowing the lawn is up, clients can decide to do more if they wish, but there is *no penalty* for doing only the one small step. Getting something done is intrinsically rewarding and encourages the low-energy client to keep on going. It also breaks the inertia, and the momentum helps them do more. Accomplishing even a small step can improve self-esteem.

John was bothered by the piles of unfiled paperwork in his office. Much of it needed to be scanned into computer files. He said it was a task that would take at least a couple of days because there was so much of it. I asked him how many minutes of scanning he

*thought he could make himself do before he would have to quit and
do something less onerous. He thought he could do 15 minutes. I
asked him at what time in the workday he thought he could do it and
he decided just before lunch because there would be a natural break
and he would not feel obligated to continue. Day by day he could get
a little done.*

Getting the Train Rolling takes this a bit further and offers
rewards for each step of finishing a project. In this technique, the
first thing to identify is how clients are spending their time—in
other words, what they *do* have the energy to do, even though they
are low on energy. Then we lay out all the steps necessary to do an
undone task, and figure out how they can do just one step before
rewarding themselves for about 15 minutes with whatever it is that
they have energy to do. In this way, tasks get done and the intrinsic rewards of accomplishment are added to the small rewards of
non-energy-consuming activity.

*John's big undone task was getting new Internet service installed
at the office. I asked John what he was doing with his time at work.
He said he drank a lot of coffee and watched news on his computer
when he felt too tired to work. So that was the activity he had enough
energy for! Now, what steps did he have to do to install the new
Internet service?*

1. List how many computers will use it
2. List how they are used (e.g., what type of data is received)
3. List which companies to call
4. Make phone calls, one at a time
5. With each call, put costs in a column to later compare
6. Choose the company

7. *Make the appointment for the work to be done*
8. *Be at the office for the appointment*
9. *Pay the bill*

Once he did just one step, he could go back to doing what he already was doing—coffee and news—for 15 minutes (set a timer!) before he returned to the next step.

Imagine Future Energy

Another way to break inertia and increase motivation is to imagine the reward of finishing something before actually doing it. Clients simply identify a task they want done, and then clearly imagine how they will feel when it is done. The task chosen should be one that is fairly easily accomplished, like paying a couple of bills (as opposed to reorganizing your finances). If clients can imagine the relief of getting those bills in the mail long enough to sit down and pay them, that relief will carry them through one small task after another. This technique works well for things like making a phone call, writing a memo or work email, emptying the dishwasher, and so on.

Enhance Positive Experiences

A critical feature of treatment is to find what brings the low-energy client pleasure and begin to build that into the model of the person's daily life. Barbara Frederickson (2001) posited the idea of "broaden and build," a way to expand positive experiences by noticing the positive aspects of an experience and exploring ways to enhance them. These positive emotions can expand our resources as well as our pleasure in life, resulting in more positive relationships and more internal resources to cope with times of distress or trouble. This is more than mindful awareness: It is about noticing, savoring, and purposefully expanding pleasures—a major issue for depressed clients in general but especially problematic for those with very low energy.

Therapy needs to start small, finding ways clients can feel pleasure without using a lot of energy. Often exploring their interests, even ones they have not pursued in some time, will provide them with ideas about what they might like to have more of. Then introduce the idea of brief exposures to the activity they might enjoy. For example, if they once enjoyed camping, you would talk together about whether they might want to have a picnic or a walk in the woods rather than a weeklong backpacking trip.

> *Jane was a perfect candidate for this technique because she had become completely out of balance, with work and more work filling her moments. But she had loved home decorating at one point, so she decided to start by spending a few minutes each morning looking at home décor websites and "pinning" her interests on the Internet so she could look at them later. Just breaking the pressure of working every minute gave a little spark to her day. Jane later enlarged that pleasure by taking a lunch break to go window-shopping for home accessories. Such activities provided her with a bit of balance as she began to intervene on her burnout.*

"Until Now"

A primary problematic thought for low-energy clients is that the condition they are in is unchangeable. Because their low energy makes it difficult for them to concentrate and imagine other options, and because their anxiety about change interferes with trying new things, they tend to get stuck in the mire of negative expectations.

A good way to change these cognitions is to simply add the words *until now* at the end of their negative statements about who they are and how their lives are. These two little words make change seem *possible* but not *mandatory*, which makes the change easier for the low-energy client to contemplate.

> *I thought the "Until Now" strategy would help John challenge his overarching cognition that things couldn't change. I asked him to add those two words when he said things like "I have always been disorganized" or "I have never loved going out with my wife's friends." I asked him to add the words regardless of whether he was speaking aloud or just thinking the thought to himself. This began to be of some use to him. Telling himself "I have been disorganized, until now . . ." allowed him to take on tasks at work that he had been avoiding, and he consequently became less agitated by his work environment. These small improvements gave him a sense of control he had not felt in a long time.*

Change Mistaken Beliefs With Education

Learning about the impact of lifestyle changes can make a remarkable difference for low-energy clients. Learning about how hard it is for the brain to change a habit, and how to change habits effectively, can relieve some of the pressure clients feel to move faster. Education about the burnout cycle of increasing isolation and harder work, as well as about the impact of denial that burnout is happening, is a vital link in changing the routine of overfocusing on work and then collapsing at home.

Consider what mistaken notions you see in your clients and offer another view through the process of education. This also helps prevent self-blame or feeling judged. Education can increase the motivation to change if clients can see that the process they are undertaking is one others have come through.

Tackle Anxiety With Planning

Having a plan requires knowing what the problem is. Many clients with low mental energy have not contemplated the nature of what is going wrong in their lives beyond administering a dose of self-blame. Not knowing what is wrong, they cannot possibly figure out what to do about it. This is often fuel for anxiety. So the first order of business is the most challenging aspect of planning: Identify the problem!

To find the problem, look for the anxiety. Low-energy clients commonly suffer from the feeling of not being "enough"—not good enough, smart enough, active enough, accomplished enough, and so on. They often feel the press of undone activities or unaccom plished goals. The feeling of needing to take action but not knowing where to start creates persistent anxiety that may be felt as a physical dread. Such anxiety can worsen the depression, and with low energy, clients find it difficult to generate optimistic visions of the future. In a way, however, the anxiety becomes helpful, because it may stimulate urgency to move. It also directs you toward a plan that will eliminate worrying and prompt action.

Anxiety tends to show itself in mental rigidity and repetition and in "what if" thinking. Listen for themes of worry that clients won't be able to accomplish goals: "There's not enough time." "What if I get sick before my test?" "What if I can't work anymore?" Anxiety about the unknown future saps energy. When you identify a goal that clients fear will be left undone, it becomes a problem they can solve. Then you can make a plan, using realistic action steps, to solve the problem. Planning helps clients see the path to accomplishment and relieves fruitless worry.

*Anxiety about unfinished business had begun to build in John.
When his wife began discussing their eventual retirement, anxiety
about having enough working years to earn the amount of money
he wanted for retirement started gnawing at him every day. He
would think about his limited time and then run in mental circles
about what to do. Things like getting a second job or changing jobs
seemed overwhelming as long as he was focused on the thought
"I need money!" He never actually defined how much money he
needed and in what amount of time. Slowing down the worry
and defining the problem more clearly was essential. Finally John
was able to see: "I want to have another full year of my current
income set aside to retire. I don't have it. I don't know what to do
and that worries me." It was then that we could begin planning
and resolve his anxiety using the following technique: Worry Well
and Only Once.*

Worry Well and Only Once

Failure to identify the problem turns planning into worrying in a
flash. When a situation has some complexity and there are steps
that may occur over an extended period of time, you want to clearly
identify the steps and the timeframe to complete them. Worry Well
and Only Once identifies all the potential glitches, problems, and
gaps in information, skills, or resources that need to be filled. Then
all the information is gathered, plans that will improve skills or gain
access to resources are made, and then worrying is declared done.
When the "oh no!" thoughts emerge later, the client is trained to
say, "Stop! I already worried!"

*John had neither consulted a financial planner nor spoken to his
wife about what needs he might have. He had not considered that
others might have information that could help. John and I made a list*

of questions he needed answers to if he were to stop feeling anxious about money and his time left to earn it. This was the "worry well" part of the plan. Getting all the concerns out in the open made it clear that there was a definable list of things to find out about. From there we figured out who could answer his questions.

A financial planner helped with exactly that. He could see what needed to happen to make sure John could meet all his obligations without running out of funds. Now, if he felt a worry about the money, he could say to himself, "Stop! I have a plan," and then do thought-replacing to move mentally away from the worry.

Planning instead of worrying is a fabulous anti-anxiety tool, and resolving ambiguity is, too. In this case, John needed to have a face-to-face, honest conversation with his wife. The idea of doing this made him anxious, but he felt relieved once he'd talked to her. He needed to put his money fears out in front and get answers so that he could stop ruminating. Having worried well and gathered the necessary information, he could, if his anxiety returned, say, "Stop! I already worried!"

ONGOING THERAPY

It may take considerable time to put all these kinds of steps in place for a low-energy client. Slowly raising the activity level to boost energy and slowly making lifestyle changes will bear fruit over months—not weeks—of time.

Encouragement during the process of changing nutrition, exercise, and other health habits will keep low-energy clients trying until they can see the results. Any client who has major lifestyle changes to make should begin slowly and try to see the small successes along the way. Keeping records may help them stay accountable, but should be done in a way that does not add to discouragement. Consider electronic options like apps on handheld devices that can let them privately keep track until they decide to whom they might want to be accountable for staying on their path to lifestyle change.

The issue of whether clients need more time to work on issues is entirely variable and based on the client's earlier life experiences. However, it is not uncommon for low-energy clients to have deeply ingrained feelings of low self-esteem surrounding their perceived failures. They often feel they should have accomplished more and may berate themselves for not pursuing opportunities that they believe are now completely lost. Insight-oriented therapy can help address these kinds of concerns. But a common theme is: "There's nothing I can do about it."

You Have Choices

Feeling as if you are making a choice gets lost with anxiety because of the incredible amount of time spent ruminating on how the situation is unalterable. "I hate my job but I can't quit because I need the money!" "I can't stand the city I'm living in but I can't move because my husband's job is here!" The truth is, however, that you are making a choice—you can quit the job if you choose to live without the money; you can move out of the city if you choose to leave your husband or have a long-distance relationship. Reframing these "no choice" statements is helpful for clients. "I can't quit the job" becomes "I won't quit the job because I want the money." "I can't move" becomes "I won't move because I want my marriage to stay intact." Encouraging clients to realize that they are making these choices helps them see their situation in a different light. They can choose to do things or stay in things, even though those choices may not be perfect. In the process of accepting that they have chosen the current situation, clients may start generating new ideas about what they might do differently to feel better. And even if that doesn't happen, knowing that they are making a choice helps them feel better about what they are doing.

A few months into therapy, John finally started to talk about missed opportunities in his life. He said he had never wanted to work in his field; he'd always wanted to teach. He had chosen his path to pay for his son's education and their nice home. He felt stuck in his current life and believed it was too late to change his path now. Framing his situation as one in which he had a choice helped a lot.

At first, of course, he said he had no choices left. "What's done is done." The road he hadn't traveled was haunting him, though. So I asked him to look seriously at what it would cost in fees and lost income to go back to school to get certified to teach. I had him look at salary differentials to see what he would make as a teacher. It did not take long to see that the costs of certification and the salary he would make as a teacher were out of balance: too high a cost for too little return. Assessing that cost of education, he determined, "I can't do that!"

Now I wanted to frame this as a choice. I asked, "Why not?"

Because he wanted the lifestyle his job afforded him, he said.

"Okay," I replied, "so you are choosing to continue in this job rather than change to teaching?"

"Well, of course," he said, sheepishly seeing my point about having made a choice.

We went on to discuss the issue. Doing the work he was doing was a choice he made every day. He could become a teacher if he wanted to. He just didn't want it enough to change his life. And staying in his current work had more benefits than downsides. This was not John being stuck. It was John preferring one outcome over another.

FINISHING UP

Many clients leave therapy when they feel things are better, even though there may still be something left undone. They may not want to do more at the time, but they almost always want to know if they can come back. You should outline the areas you think they might want to work on more at another time, and indicate that with their successes so far, they might resolve those things, too, without therapy.

I think it is reassuring to let clients know they can come back anytime, for one session or several, to talk about an issue. There is a lot to be gained by talking with someone who knows you well and can reflect with you on your situation.

> *After 15 months of therapy with John, I still saw some unresolved issues with his self-esteem and his marriage, but he was ready to be done. I commented that his sex life was still an unresolved area in his marriage, but because neither he nor his wife currently were expressing distress about it, it was not the time to work on it. I may see him again in the future for an issue of that type, but he thinks he is doing much better overall. He had accomplished the goal of getting mobilized, less depressed, and less anxious.*

TREATMENT SUMMARY FOR THE LOW-ENERGY CLIENT

Assessment

- Physical health—consider a medical assessment of sleep, vitamin D, thyroid, iron deficiencies and other causes of low energy
- Readiness to change—assess positive motivations about what is to be gained by treatment; assess negative motivations, especially if the client is being pushed into therapy

- Mental energy—initial steps must be slow; starting with a motivational interviewing style will engage clients in a way that creates mental preparation to move

Therapeutic Relationship
Clients are sensitive to being judged or pushed too fast. Focus strongly on acceptance, support, and collaborative decision-making about treatment steps.

Addressing the Symptoms
Assess need for lifestyle changes such as sufficient exercise and good nutrition. Changes occur slowly and lead to eventual improvement. Encouragement is necessary; focus the client's attention on successful small changes to keep movement going.

Specific Therapy Tools for Change
- Prime the Pump
- Get the Train Rolling
- Imagine Future Energy
- Enhance Positive Experiences
- "Until Now" (to counter negative beliefs)
- Change Mistaken Beliefs With Education
- Tackle Anxiety With Planning (identify the problem by looking at anxiety and then make steps to solve it)
- Worry Well and Only Once

Ongoing Therapy
- Changes occur slowly—focus on noticing success; be encouraging
- You Have Choices (staying or leaving is in your control)

Finishing Up

- State confidence in client's achievements to date and identify possible areas for later therapy
- Invite client to return at any time, even if just for a session or two

CHAPTER 4

THE HOPELESS RUMINATOR

HOPELESS RUMINATORS present with worry that is negative in tone, a sad demeanor, and depression showing in feelings of failure or hopelessness that they can change. The following checklist indicates the main characteristics of hopeless ruminators.

||||||||||||||||||||||||||||||||||||||||||||||||||||||||||||||||||||||||||||

_____ *Persistent worry.* The client may complain more about anxiety as a troubling symptom than about depression, because persistent worry over everyday life situations is not responsive to reassurance or cognitive control methods.

_____ *Hopeless attitude and negative expectations.* The client may harbor some small hope that things could improve, but the overall view of life is pessimistic and the client does not expect his or her efforts to produce change.

_____ *Sense of duty or heightened responsibility.* The client meets work responsibilities but is rarely enthusiastic or energetic and performs with strong sense of duty.

_____ *Restrained anger.* The client does not express anger openly and may be passive aggressive when afraid of losing a relationship if the client were to speak up.

_____ *External locus of control.* The client is moody and worried about choices yet perceives many decisions to be the result of other people's influence or needs.

_____ *Difficulty describing the quality of one's overall emotional and physical state.* The vague statement "I feel bad" is frequently offered by clients to express their persistent negative physical and mental agitation.

|||||||||||||||||||||||||||||||||||||||||||||||||||||||||||||||||||||||||

Of all the client types I describe, it is the hopeless ruminator who is most likely to appear depressed but complain about anxiety. Just as you are listening to how worry plagues this person's every waking moment and you become convinced it is a case of generalized anxiety disorder, you hear the hopelessness well up. Then these clients sound depressed and ready to quit whatever situation they think there is no solution for. As a therapist I find myself challenged to stay optimistic about treatment with these clients, who can initially seem "on board" to try out cognitive tools but later tell you there is no way the method will do enough good. They do not see how treatment is going to help. They feel their worries are insurmountable, even when they know the worry is unfounded.

Hopeless ruminators probably are born with a genetic predisposition to mood disorders, with life circumstances provoking the emergence of the depression and anxiety. These clients may have been depressed first or anxious first (which you may be able to discern from listening to their history) but they will present in therapy with both disorders in evidence.

One common element among these clients who seem depressed but worry constantly is they often exhibit an external locus of control, meaning that others have strong influence on their internal state of wellbeing. Another common thread in the life histories of hopeless ruminators is parental relationships that were emotionally distant or decidedly unsupportive but not abusive by standard definitions. The client as a child may have been confused about how to obtain attention or approval, but the problem connection with parents was not severe enough to be considered an attachment failure. Children can learn to worry from parents, and this seems to be the case with the hopeless ruminators I have worked with. Their parents modeled negativity and worry and in many cases did not expect or demand good treatment from the world around them.

The biggest challenge in working with these clients is addressing the way their inability to hope affects their follow-through with therapy. Although they appear to need support—and they *do* need it—supportive psychotherapy alone does not offer them ideas to manage their anxiety. Their hopelessness may not be as deep as that of those who are solely depressed and deeply hopeless (as in depression from attachment disorder) but it nevertheless exacerbates their tendency toward having an external locus of control and they may not believe treatment will work. These clients will wait passively for you to offer (at last!) a magic idea to help them feel better instead of actively trying out many ideas to see what has the best result.

In these cases you will find yourself weaving back and forth between anxiety and depression management techniques, and that is to be expected. Because of the depressive aspect of these clients' ruminating worry, you may need to start with smaller steps than their otherwise "willing to work" demeanor might suggest.

A CASE OF THE HOPELESS RUMINATOR

Terese, age 41, came to see me because she felt overwhelmed by anxiety about parenting. During our first session she seemed distracted, and she paused for long periods while speaking and sighed a lot. Her daughter was entering her teens and Terese couldn't stop worrying that she wouldn't turn out all right. Terese's partner disagreed with many of her attempts to discipline their daughter, telling Terese to "lighten up" and not take everything so seriously. This made her feel as if she was doing something wrong, but she also felt scared because she didn't know how her daughter would learn to be responsible if she was always let off the hook for not getting schoolwork and chores done. When there had been a disagreement, Terese couldn't relax and enjoy reading or watching television until she found a way to mollify whoever was mad. She felt defeated and said she was tired of "giving in" to her partner and her daughter but didn't know what else she could do. "This is not the way I thought it would be to have a family," she lamented. She said her home life was tolerable when everything was peaceful, but she was always edgy, waiting for someone to be mad at her. "This suffering is getting old!" she said. "I want to stop it."

When I asked Terese about her own upbringing, she described her parents as completely uninvolved except for occasional, unpredictable screaming at her for "infractions." Her mother worked a physical job and was always tired when she was home. Her father was often lost in his drinking, so while they were there, they were not really pres-

ent. Terese's grades were good and she did not get into trouble. "I was too afraid to make a mistake, so there was no way I was going to do things I knew were wrong." Terese looked sad and periodically stared into space when she was thinking about how to answer. She seemed hyperaware of how I was reacting to her story, and often prefaced her remarks with, "I know you are going to think I am _____ (bad, wrong, stupid, weak, and so on)." She said she wanted to do more for herself, like eat right and exercise and take care of her house, but it seemed like too much effort while she was so preoccupied with her home life.

ASSESSMENT

During assessment, a major goal is to discover the degree of energy these clients can bring to their recovery. The agitation may be sapping their energy but it may be possible to redirect it, so looking for arenas where they feel hopeful and optimistic will comprise part of the assessment. Of course, these clients are as likely as others to have general health concerns and should have a physical before treatment. Their anxiety may not be caused by the condition of their general health, but because this client complains of feeling bad, a checkup is never a bad idea!

Physical Health

There is no particular health issue to be watchful of with the hopeless ruminator, but, depending on the intensity of the rumination, be alert to the possibility of:

- *Latent food allergies.* Not all food allergies result in anaphylaxis. As noted earlier, one of the indicators of a latent food allergy is a strong preference for and constant eating of that food. Other indicators include throat-clearing following the food consumption, digestive problems that may include irritable bowel, and problems losing weight. All of these may be signs of other issues, but they are worth considering as possible indications of food allergy.

- *Poor nutrition or need for supplements to boost neurotransmitter production.* Supplements such as omega-3, SAMe, folate, 5-HTP, and L-tryptophan can improve brain function. As a therapist, I do not tell clients to take any specific medication or supplement, as I'm not sufficiently trained to make such recommendations. However, I point out that clients may have nutrition deficiencies and I provide resources and referrals for them to pursue should they choose to.

Terese had recently gotten vaccinations and a physical, as required by her job at a hospital lab. She said she was about 20 pounds overweight but her health was otherwise pretty good. I knew we would eventually need to address nutrition and exercise as part of becoming less depressed and anxious, but there were no urgent health issues.

Readiness to Change

Hopeless ruminators typically have two stumbling blocks in their readiness to change. The first is that they don't believe they can be different. This is rooted in the ruminative worry that besets them: Most of their thoughts revolve around (and around) what is wrong or scary or potentially troublesome. Because they feel they cannot control this thought process, they cannot imagine how they will change it. But the fact that they came to therapy is evidence of some small hope.

The second stumbling block has to do with why they want to change. It is not unusual for hopeless ruminators to want to please someone else, and they may enter treatment in order to make some-one else happy. That's not the worst motivation in the world, but it can sabotage recovery if the client does not have a personal desire to feel better. Passive aggressiveness may crop up with hopeless rumi-nators, as it's their way of showing that they don't have to please others without having to be assertive. Fortunately, this behavior is fairly easy to identify and shift to self-motivation.

Terese came to therapy on her own accord, and she expressed a desire to change her behavior as well as to make herself less troubled by her home relationships. She said her partner would like it if she could relax and be happier. When asked if she had that as a personal goal, she replied, "Why wouldn't I want that?" Even if she did want to be happier, it was possible that she also resented "having to change" to satisfy her partner, in which case she might sabotage recovery to prove her partner didn't have all the power. We would return to the issue of personal motivation at many points in treatment.

Mental Energy

The very intensity of the hopeless ruminator's worry reflects a lot of mental activity. That activity can be harnessed and used in treatment, but it isn't easy, because worrying consumes these clients' energy and their hopelessness causes them to give up easily when faced with a challenge. Therapy must capitalize on clients' mental energy by redi-recting it toward solution-generating thoughts whenever possible.

Terese received good evaluations at work. Home was a different story. She had ideas about how to discipline her daughter (grounding her for missing curfew, taking the phone away for not doing home-work), but she felt defeated before she even started, knowing she would be overruled by her partner. It was this "giving up" aspect of her men-tal energy that I wanted to keep an eye on. I hoped to help her mobilize

*the energy she already had, evidenced in her ability to generate good
ideas about discipline, to help her find the will to not give up, whether
it was about discipline or managing her anxiety and depression.*

THERAPEUTIC RELATIONSHIP

The hopeless ruminator is going to be on guard for disapproval. As
their histories often include shaky attachment relationships with
parents and years of feeling depressed or not good enough, these
clients may well want to please the therapist, too. Wishing to be
perceived as good clients, they may overreport improvement or offer
praise of the therapist.

Often there is a therapeutic temptation to be so supportive of
these clients, and so accepting of a slow pace in treatment, that we
inadvertently undermine their confidence in their own self-effec-
tiveness. We may give the message that we do not expect them to
change their situations quickly. Avoiding this trap means putting
the means of change in their hands without taking away support.
One way to do that is with information. Educating them about the
way the brain, possibly low on neurotransmitters, might perceive too
much negativity, have trouble accessing positive memory, and tend
toward repetitive worry may help hopeless ruminators acknowledge
their problem without self-blame. Such education can offer hope
that change is possible and puts the power to change in their hands
if they are willing to alter their health conditions and boost brain
function.

*Terese was passive enough that I worried that she would view
therapy assignments as too much expectation. I wanted to have
expectations but also make them small enough not to overwhelm*

her. For example, when we talked about parenting, I wanted to affirm that she could be a stronger parent yet I did not want her to feel she had to change everything that she hoped to change all at once. I suggested that we first would look at what she already knew about parenting skills and make a list of things she thought were important to discipline, and then gradually try to introduce them. For example, instead of grounding her daughter from the cellphone for a weekend but then giving in when her partner disagreed, Terese could deny her access to the cellphone for 20 minutes while they ate dinner.

Additionally, with every desired change also comes the loss of what we walk away from. Clients must be ready to leave what was— if they aren't, it can be a hindrance in their progress.

This turned out to be a big problem for Terese. She identified her fear that if she pushed for her own ideas about parenting, her partner might walk away. If she became stronger, she might not have someone to rely on. We addressed this over time in several straightforward conversations about what she valued about her relationship and what it cost her emotionally to stay in the relationship.

A different pattern is evident in the hopeless ruminator who is entirely ready to change but still gives up easily because of expectation of failure. This was the case with Riley.

Riley, 31, had recently been promoted to a supervisor position at the marketing firm where she worked. She came to therapy because the promotion had caused her anxiety to worsen. "I just feel bad all the time," Riley said. "When I think about work, I feel bad. I feel bad even when I'm with friends. I try to cover it up so I won't interfere with their fun, but I know I'm probably spoiling their night anyway." She ruminated about her failures constantly, fearing she wouldn't be able to fulfill work responsibilities and feeling like a fraud for having gotten the new position in the first place. Every day at work offered a new opportunity to castigate herself. Riley looked very anxious on the surface, with worry as the dominant symptom, but the underlying themes had to do with hopelessness: "I'll never be good enough. I will fail and then I'll never get another good job."

However, unlike Terese, Riley saw no downside to change. She knew her friends would cheer if she could "stop being down on" herself, and she'd make a better impression at work if she seemed more self-confident.

ADDRESSING THE SYMPTOMS

With hopeless ruminators, changes should be brought into treatment with the plan to make them small shifts that are likely to succeed. An area to promote change is in strengthening clients' connections to people who will support them in the process.

Lifestyle

Lifestyle changes may not be necessary, unless you observe a particular problem, such as a need for exercise, better nutrition, or stress-management skills.

Support Groups

Support groups can be of enormous help to hopeless ruminators. Their mental energy will be constantly redirected to ideas for positive change, and this can boost confidence in recovery, creating hope to combat the depressed side of their makeup. Consider 12-step programs, especially those for family members of substance abusers, or find community groups for parenting, grieving, divorce, or living with some type of mental or physical illness in themselves or family members.

> *Because Terese was mostly worried about her parenting choices, she found a parent support group that bolstered her confidence in herself when her partner was nay-saying her ideas. She was able to redirect her mental energy toward generating options to intervene in her daughter's negative behaviors.*

Specific Therapy Tools for Change

With hopeless ruminators it is wise to start change with tools that depend on the client's own actions or thoughts. Changing attitudes and actions in ways that will not elicit resistance from family or other significant people will be more successful and will allow clients to strengthen their emotional resilience before tackling change that will affect their relationships with others.

Differentiate Between Control and Influence

Countless people try to control other people's behavior, mood, or emotions despite the fact that doing so is impossible. (Just try to control whether a baby will fall asleep or stop crying!) In struggling to control, they overlook the fact that they may be able to influence another person's choices. Influence is entirely in one's own hands—even though the outcome of those efforts to influence isn't. Differentiating between control and influence is a way to shift the locus of control from being external toward being internal, which helps to reduce anxiety. Explore whatever arenas of life your clients want to control and examine what they might be able to do with their own behavior to influence outcomes.

Terese often complained that she couldn't overrule her partner and couldn't control her daughter. I agreed with her, but I encouraged her to think about how she had influence, even if she wasn't currently using it. For example, if her daughter spoke to her disrespectfully, Terese's current response was to say, over and over, "This has to stop!" or "I can't believe you said that!" When I asked, "What does it mean to not believe it?" Terese said, "I did not raise her to be like that. How can she talk to her mother that way?" Her hopelessness prevented her from thinking about what she actually wanted to do about the situation.

I then asked Terese how she could exert influence on her daughter to stop arguing. "Well, I could leave the room, and then she would not be able to talk to me," she replied. She could see how that would influence the argument! The retreat was tactical, a time to regroup. It was a small change that therefore was doable.

Terese knew she had enough control over her own behavior to stop the arguing by walking away. She could not control her daughter's mouth, but she did not have to listen to it, either. Influencing the arguing by not engaging in it, Terese could relax her mind and body and consider her next steps.

Move Your Body, Move Your Mind

Breaking old patterns of behavior is actually a brain-based challenge. Educate your clients that behavior habits are ingrained in brain circuits, and to disengage from them, people need to both plan new behavior and give their brains a chance to shift gears before they fall into their old pattern. No patterns are eliminated overnight. Brains slowly develop new habits that override old habits, but the old habits die hard. Two things make introducing new actions easier:

- Create a space before responding (so the new actions can emerge). This might be literal space, but often a space of time is enough.
- Move the body, which will help the mind to shift.

It is not uncommon for people with anxiety to feel frozen and have trouble solving problems in the moment, and it helps to give them both time and physical movement to enhance their mental flexibility and break out of an old habit of responding. Often movement will provide both.

> *Terese needed to shake out of her shocked "I can't believe it" mode. Getting out of the room gave her time to think, but she also needed to shift her mind to a more influential response. She thought she could walk the dog or just walk around the block.*

Turn "I Can't" Into "I Won't"

This strategy addresses the hopeless ruminator's fixation on external locus of control. It is necessary to directly address these clients' hopeless attitude that nothing will change by first taking charge of language. It is absolutely true that we believe what we tell ourselves, and saying "I can't" is a sure way to fail. Therapy that focuses on this simple linguistic shift from "I can't" to "I won't" involves weaving the change into the many conversations that occur from session to session. Every time clients make a statement of "I can't" ("I can't make myself exercise, eat better, stick to my guns about discipline, go back to school, earn more money, etc.") you simply suggest that they instead say "I won't" and continue their sentence. Then check in on how that feels to them.

Clients' first response is often "But I want to do it! I just can't." I briefly explain the importance of this language change, and then

I ask them again to state "I won't" and go on. I inquire about where the power to change lies when they say "I won't." This is the essential shift that promotes changing the locus of control. Of course, locus of control is generally a deeper issue, but changing it can start here.

When I asked Terese to substitute "I won't" for "I can't," she immediately asked what good it would do. I told her we would just pay attention in therapy and see what happened. It didn't take long for the first practice opportunity to come up:

"I can't keep track of my daughter's homework when my partner tells me to leave her alone."

Try, "I won't . . ."

"But I can't! They get mad at me."

Try, "I won't . . ."

"Okay, then. I won't keep track of her homework when my partner tells me to leave her alone."

When I asked Terese what it felt like to say "I won't," she explained that she'd always felt hopeless about getting her partner and daughter to cooperate, and always felt like she was giving in. Saying "I won't" gave her the sense that she could personally make a choice to let it go and let the two of them deal with the consequences. She moved the control back into herself. And it felt pretty good! We kept up this way of intervening in sessions for several weeks until it was automatic.

Change Your Explanatory Style

Hopeless ruminators actively repeat negative explanations of life circumstances, and these explanations entrench their attitude of hopelessness and foster their passivity. They may tell themselves that they are weak, or that others do not love them, or they have no luck, or any number of other self-defeating messages. Therapists should listen to these ruminative explanations and, with the client's cooperation, write a new script to deliberately replace the negative rumination.

It was quite clear that Terese was running a dialogue in her mind about how no one valued her opinion and there was no point in trying. After we talked about changing this script, Terese decided to tell herself that she had good ideas about parenting and they had all gotten in the habit of not listening to one another.

What's the Disaster?

This tool to change the conceptualization of the problem is used in many different ways in treating anxiety and depression. Over-reactions are often based in faulty perceptions of the severity of a problem, and clients' hopeless passivity contributes to this faulty perception. This simple intervention nudges clients in the direction of evaluating whether their circumstances are actually as bad as they feel they are. The key is to get clients to recognize that there is not a disaster; they just do not like what is happening. That recognition immediately lessens overreactions and lowers stress.

I wanted to nudge Terese to evaluate why she was reacting so strongly to her daughter's disrespectful behavior. In asking herself what the disaster was, she could immediately see there was none. What she was worrying about was a far distant issue: "How will my daughter be as an adult if I let her treat me this way now?" That is an important question about an important issue, but there was no immediate disaster.

Modulate Your Response

If there is no disaster, then the response to a situation can be less intense, too. Again, look at the language used to describe the internal state. "I am furious!" "I am so insulted!" "How dare she treat me that way?" "She never supports me—it's always about her!" "If this doesn't change she will ruin her life!" Statements of extreme emotionality and "always" or "never" terminology will rev up emotions further. It is best to modulate the verbal response and try to calm down behavior as well.

> Terese's responses to her daughter are great examples of this. She needed to tone down her outrage and her fear because she was reacting to her own tone of voice. Instead of using big, all-or-nothing words, she could tell herself she was "irritated, not outraged," or that "just because her homework is not done by 7 P.M. does not mean she will fail high school in 5 years." This helped Terese modulate her response: "If she texts too much I do not have to take her phone away entirely. I can take her phone away while she does homework or overnight." Being less extreme about her descriptions and responses modulated Terese's emotional tone, as well as her behavior in disciplining her daughter.

Some clients are more depressed in their cognitions and loop negative thinking in a way that intensifies the depression. Self-criticism and ruminating about failure can be exaggerated in hopeless ruminators, especially when their depression preceded their anxiety.

"What Can I Control Now, What Can I Control Later, and What Can I Never Control?"

These three questions immediately modulate both emotion and behavior by separating the time frames and the range of genuine influence clients may have in changing their circumstance. Asking oneself what aspects of a situation are in one's immediate control requires a person to evaluate whether an actual problem exists at the moment. Actual problems that exist in the moment are distinguished from potential problems that have not yet occurred, and this automatically calms the immediate reaction.

Asking oneself what can be controlled *later* implies that *if* a problem arises, it can be handled when it does; thus, instead of worrying now, when the problem may never arise, one focuses on what can be done to cope with the possible future problem.

Finally, remembering that some things will never be in our control reins in the sensation that we *must* be in charge of everything, irrational as that idea may be! The separation of these three aspects of a situation instantly scales down behavior responses.

Riley used this method to modulate her self-criticism one day for "overreacting" in a meeting. She was fretting that, as a new supervisor, she had "ruined the discussion" and "stifled creativity" when one colleague raised an objection to a team goal. She asked herself the following questions:

- What can I control now? Nothing. It is done. I wasn't wrong in what I did, just perhaps too peremptory. Stop worrying. (See the Thought-Stopping method in Chapter 9).
- What can I control later? At the next meeting, I can make an effort to handle the discussion differently and allow more room for others to give input. I don't have to keep thinking about this now.
- What will I never be able to control? I cannot control what others think or how they say things.

ONGOING THERAPY

It takes time for behavior to change, and therapy must include conversations about trying to suspend self-criticism when change is slow. Education about habits can be reiterated as well.

> *It took about 6 months before Terese could reliably exert self-control and supplant the old habit of expressing shock and outrage with walking away and doing effective problem-solving. Realizing that old habits take time to fade, she became less judgmental of herself.*

Discuss Relationship Changes

Because they may have relationships in which they have maintained a passive role, hopeless ruminators may find that those relationships begin to change when they start being a bit more confident or assertive. Often these changes are for the better, and clients need to observe these positive changes.

They can also observe if the relationship suffers from their confident stance and discuss what impact that has on their progress. If they are prone to passive aggressiveness, that behavior will often emerge more at this point. When therapy can focus on specific examples of their passive-aggressive behavior, clients can be helped to note the outcome of it. They will be more able to see that it is ineffective because they are evaluating behavior and outcome on an ongoing basis.

> *As Terese developed some ability to walk away and take charge of her own emotions, she felt less at the mercy of her family's actions and more able to make some choices of her own. As she predicted, tension rose with her partner, but now she could identify her own passive ways of showing anger. For example, one morning Terese did not*

mention that she would have to stay late at work that day. When no one was home to give their daughter a ride to a school activity, both the daughter and Terese's partner were upset. Terese tried to justify her actions with "it wasn't my fault—I had to work!" which allowed her to indulge her feelings of frequently being taken for granted or taken advantage of. As we discussed this incident, Terese saw the passive-aggressive quality of her own behavior and how it was more hostile than assertive. As she saw how fruitless and infuriating her actions were, Terese felt more control to change her own behavior. She could now work directly on standing up for her own needs appropriately.

Focus on Health

Hopeless ruminators may have been letting health issues like nutrition or exercise go, and this can be a time to introduce attention to those areas to promote overall recovery. Excuses often fall into the category of not having time or needing to spend their energy on other people. That external locus of control will have interfered with self-care. For example, some clients will not make healthful meals if they think no one else will eat them. Encouraging them by stressing that self-care improves one's ability to care for others is one way to improve habits.

After some discussion, Terese decided to start taking the dog for long walks (good for the dog as well as herself) and inviting her daughter or partner to accompany her so she did not feel that she was deserting them. The dog had to get out and she could defend this self-care to herself because she had been willing to include others.

Journaling

Making changes stick may mean gaining insight into what purposes the anxiety has served (for example, getting reassurance from others) or how the depression began, such as a reaction to feeling persistently alone. There is no one issue you will see here, but, obviously, when there have been troubled parental relationships from early on, they will have an impact. Insight alone won't make change happen, but it can help solidify changes and maintain them. Journaling is a helpful tool to explore these childhood experiences that influence self-esteem, locus of control, and models for worry and negativity ingrained by parents.

Emotions often trigger anxiety so fast that the emotion gets swallowed up by the anxiety and is missed entirely. A way to get back to that original emotion and identify why it is anxiety provoking is to ask what physical sensation comes up when the client is thinking about the situation. One journaling method that works well is having clients ask themselves a series of questions aimed at connecting *current* feelings or actions to *earlier* feelings (rather than trying to remember specific situations), trying to develop an image about when physical sensations related to the anxiety first occurred. Clients are asked to notice where in the body sensations occur and to give them a physical description. Then clients ask themselves:

- What is the earliest age I remember having this physical feeling?
- What was happening when I had it? (The past situation they remember here may not be similar to the current situation. There may only be a snapshot-like image, but it can be fleshed out in conversation or writing—who was present, what might have been happening, and so on.)
- What emotions might be associated with that situation?
- Is that in any way like what I am feeling now?

Terese tried this method when she got intensely anxious after her partner took their daughter shopping for a new outfit despite Terese's having already said that the daughter couldn't have a new outfit. She started by identifying the physical sensation—a "frozen feeling" in her chest. Trying to remember the earliest age she had this feeling, Terese immediately recalled a time when she was 7 years old and sitting on the stairs in her family home. Fleshing it out, she remembered that her mother and sister were trying on a new dress for her sister. Terese had felt left out and jealous. Once she brought this to awareness, the parallels were obvious, but she could also see how the situation today was not the same. Now she could plan a different reaction.

FINISHING UP

There will be times when hopeless ruminators appropriately transition into family or couples counseling, as their behaviors may affect those relationships. They may especially benefit from longer-term work on locus-of-control issues, which can come up in subtler ways and prevent ongoing self-care, prompt increased passive-aggressive behavior, or interfere with advancing at work if they wait for others to notice or approve of their achievements.

TREATMENT SUMMARY FOR THE HOPELESS RUMINATOR

Assessment

Physical health—consider the possibility of food allergy as well as the need for supplementing nutrition with omega-3, SAMe, folate, 5-HTP, L-tryptophan, or other supplements that help the brain to establish healthy levels of neurotransmitters

Readiness to change—watch for the two possible stumbling blocks (lack of belief that change is possible, and seeking treatment just to make someone else happy); education about brain-based causes of anxiety and depression and about change is helpful

Mental energy—capitalize on clients' mental energy by redirecting it toward solution-generating thoughts

Therapeutic Relationship

Clients are on guard for approval or disapproval due to external locus of control. Watch out for the therapeutic pitfall of being too supportive and not expecting enough. Keep an eye out for passive-aggressive behavior in the therapy as well as in the client's personal relationships.

Addressing the Symptoms

There are no lifestyle problems to address other than the typical issues of nutrition and exercise that affect most therapy clients. Stress is usually more from clients' own attitudes than from life circumstances, but offer stress-management help when necessary.

Support Groups

Support or education groups can bolster confidence, offer hope, and redirect mental energy toward solution-generating rather than worrying.

Specific Therapy Tools for Change
- Differentiate Between Control and Influence
- Move Your Body, Move Your Mind (find ways to shift the stuck brain by shifting the body)
- Turn "I Can't" Into "I Won't" (addresses locus-of-control issues)

- Change Your Explanatory Style (write a different script about problem situations)
- What's the Disaster?
- Modulate Your Response
- "What Can I Control Now, What Can I Control Later, and What Can I Never Control?

Ongoing Therapy
- Discuss relationship changes
- Focus on health
- Journal (encourage insight by identifying the physical sensation and how it is like one experienced in a childhood situation)

Finishing Up
- Couples or family counseling
- Locus-of-control work to deal with passive aggressiveness and poor self-care

CHAPTER 5

THE PANICKY & DEPRESSED CLIENT

THESE CLIENTS are often only mildly depressed, and they may not even become aware of their depression until after they begin therapy for their panic attacks. Because the panic is a more unfamiliar and disturbing symptom, they focus on getting for treatment for that, but when the therapy begins it becomes evident that the pessimistic outlook has been present for a long time. Probably endogenous, the depression usually has developed slowly over many years. The following checklist indicates the main characteristics of the panicky and depressed client.

|||||||||||||||||||||||||||||||||||||||||||||||||||||||||||||||||||||||

———— *Mild to moderate depression symptoms.* The client will usually seek therapy for panic attacks rather than for depression.

———— *Passive personality.* This may mask depression in a client who is naturally less socially involved and talks less about emotions.

_____   *Introversion.* Even when socially capable, the client is exhausted by too much "other people time" and by work meetings.

_____   *Panic attacks initially triggered by unexpected situational stress.* The client may have experienced his or her first panic attack in the wake of a sudden loss, a difficult situation at work, or an unexpected health problem.

_____   *Panic following overreaction to stress.* This leads to bad decisions about life problems and hasty reactions while panicky.

_____   *Less participation in previously enjoyed activities to avoid panic.* Initially withdrawing from life to avoid panic, the client has fewer fun, joyful experiences and becomes depressed.

_____   *Difficulty accomplishing work or personal goals due to panic.* The client may have begun to avoid situations that might cause panic, which interferes with work and personal life.

_____   *Pessimism about outcomes to situations.* This leads to overreactivity.

_____   *Pessimism about overcoming anxiety and stress.* As depression emerges, the client has less hope that he or she will feel better.

||||||||||||||||||||||||||||||||||||||||||||||||||||||||||||||||||||||

When clients with depression—even mild or moderate depression—develop panic, their depression worsens. People who suffer panic disorder without depression *can* feel calm and undisturbed when they are confident that they can avoid a panic attack. In between attacks, they may not feel depressed or even anxious, and they only worry about when they will panic next so they can plan how to avoid it. When they are certain they are in a safe place, their emotions can be placid. When depression is added to the picture, however, panic becomes a hard emotional state from which to recover. The depression adds to a constant feeling of discouragement and distress, making people have less relief between bouts of panic, causing them to need more reassurance, and diminishing their courage to face the panic.

As I mentioned earlier, the mild to moderate depression in these cases has usually existed for a long time, and clients often don't know exactly when it started. However, the panic attacks usually are prompted by a major, unexpected situational stress. Once that panic is introduced, the depression deepens and panic disorder quickly develops because these clients are not resilient in the face of such intense and sudden anxiety.

A CASE OF THE PANICKY AND DEPRESSED CLIENT

Shannon, age 34, was a middle-school teacher who came to therapy presenting with panic attacks. Her panic was triggered whenever someone began talking about students committing suicide. The previous year, a student in one of her classes had committed suicide, and there had been a number of suicides in recent months at other schools. The spate of deaths was a topic of great concern among her colleagues, and when they discussed signs of suicidality, Shannon had a panic attack at the thought that she might be at fault for not seeing signs. Although no one ever suggested she could have done more for the student in her class, she had begun panicking whenever that thought crossed her mind. After the deaths, Shannon had stopped joining other teachers for lunch because she "needed a break" from the talk about the suicides, but in the last couple of weeks her avoidance had become more extreme: She now

*stayed away entirely from the teacher's lounge in an effort to pre-
vent another panic attack.*

*Shannon also complained of ongoing exhaustion. She said she
couldn't imagine socializing with other teachers during nonworking hours because she'd had enough contact with them in the course
of a school day and in extracurricular events. She also told me she
might have been depressed on and off all her life because, like her
mother, she always felt self-critical and thought others were better
at everything than she was. She was not suicidal, but she told me
she thought about killing herself whenever she felt panicky. "I don't
know why it seems like a solution then, when I don't feel that bad
all the time, but I can't think of any other way to get rid of the bad
feelings."*

ASSESSMENT

Concerns about physical health are certainly on the mind of the
panicky and depressed client, who finds it hard to believe there is
not a health-related cause of the panic: heart issues or worse! Such
health problems certainly need to be ruled out, and once they are,
treatment can begin by directing clients' attention to panic-fueling
lifestyle issues over which they have control.

Physical Health

Panicky and depressed clients have often addressed their health
issues quite thoroughly because panic attacks have brought them to
a physician. However, it is wise to review for the following common
potential causes or triggers for panic.

- *Caffeine consumption.* Caffeine can hide in medications
  and many foods. Some people's genetic makeup predis-

poses them to caffeine-triggered panic attacks; for others, raising the level of physiological stimulation makes panic more likely.

- *Sugar.* An hour or so after consuming a large dose of sugar, such as a candy bar, some people will feel hot, queasy, or shaky. People who panic may interpret these feelings as the beginning of a panic attack, which then actually brings one on.
- *Alcohol.* Consuming large amounts of alcohol can bring on panic many hours after the end of the alcohol consumption, when people no longer connect panic with the drinking. Check for the consumption of large amounts of alcohol.
- *Medication side effects.* Many medications can produce the symptoms of panic, especially steroids such as prednisone and asthma medications.
- *Hormone fluctuations.* With female clients, check whether panic is associated with monthly cycles. One caveat here: If your client is a woman with depression and she has her first panic attack after menopause, she needs a careful cardiac evaluation. It is possible that the panic attack is not panic but rather a warning signal of a future cardiac event.

Shannon was in good physical condition and was taking care of herself because she wanted to get pregnant. She worked out nearly every day, and her weight and nutrition were fairly sound. The biggest issue was migraine headaches that would sideline her for a day or two. She was on no medication other than headache medication as needed.

Readiness to Change

Most people with panic are eager to eliminate their attacks, and unless they are receiving some big secondary gain from the attacks (like getting attention) they see the problem as their own and want to stop suffering. The only interference may come from the helpless feelings some people develop because panic makes them feel out of control and they have had no success in stopping it.

> *Shannon seemed motivated and ready to let go of her panic. There was no obvious way that it was helping her. But she also had negative expectations of herself. She was not accustomed to feeling good about herself, and her inability to control the panic made her feel even less capable and lowered her self-esteem.*

Mental Energy

Because their depression is usually mild or moderate, these clients have sufficient mental energy to learn and apply panic-management tools. In fact, learning that they can eliminate their panic attacks or at least minimize their suffering from them increases their positive mood and counteracts depression. But when panic hits, it tends to reinforce depression. These clients feel that they can't control their panic, which engenders helplessness and, thus, low self-esteem. The more depressed they become, the more they avoid situations in order to avoid panic. It is helpful to explore this interaction between depression and feelings of helplessness with these clients.

> *We wanted to know what started Shannon's cycle of panic and depression. Her mental energy fluctuated: When she was feeling fairly good, she seemed to have an abundance of energy and*

exerted efforts to identify and control her panic. When she felt more depressed, she lost mental focus and did not do much to minimize her panic attacks. The panic would then increase her depression and a circular reinforcement of symptoms would occur. She often ended up with a migraine at these times. Exploring the onset of these headaches helped us identify the events that got the cycle started by triggering the depression or anxiety. Shannon noticed, for example, that conflicts with her colleagues and knocks to her self-esteem (such as a recent snub by a school administrator at a school-related social event) prompted depressed feelings and made it more likely that she would panic. Shannon found she could actually improve her mood by practicing panic management.

The situational stress that starts the panic may also be the trigger for future panic attacks. Knowing what initially triggered the panic is critical to treating it. Whereas some clients may have a panic attack after suffering an imagined guilt, others may develop panic as the outcome of a real mistake. Clients in this latter group may respond faster to treatment because they can work on a real situation and figure out how to prevent it from happening again. Clients like Shannon, who are beset by guilt despite the absence of any clear wrongdoing, struggle more with their ability to accurately perceive life events, and this makes them vulnerable to finding new causes to panic.

Another client, Roger, sought therapy 3 years after his first panic attack, which was had resulted from a situation in which he really was at fault. Roger had been struggling to get along with a new boss who was demanding more meetings and more "drive along" time with Roger to his appointments with clients. In a moment of high frustration during a meeting, Roger blurted out, "Maybe I should just leave!" and to his shock, his boss agreed. Roger was unemployed before he fully realized what had happened. His panic attacks began that day and continued for 3 years, increasing in severity until he decided he needed treatment. He had a new job, and it was going well, but he still felt such intense anxiety that whenever he was asked to speak up or present data at a meeting, he froze, panicked, and could not speak.

Although he admitted to never having been a particularly optimistic person, Roger said that depression had not been a problem for him prior to the emergence of his panic. As the panic attacks continued, however, and as he felt increasingly powerless to stop them, Roger became more and more despondent. By the time he sought treatment, the circular reinforcement between his depression and panic was profound.

Introversion

A special consideration in mental energy is related to introversion and the way it affects people's capacity for energetic responses. Introversion in this kind of client may be something of a surprise if the client has the appearance of being outgoing. But clients can be friendly and socially competent yet still find that social interaction uses up their store of energy. Being around other people can be exhausting for these clients, and they may need to regroup to prevent depression from intensifying.

Shannon's description of needing lunchtimes alone and being constantly exhausted (yet having the energy to work out) seemed to indicate introversion. For Roger, talking to the people on his accounts was something he could manage, but his new boss's strategy of being very involved verbally and in person exhausted Roger's reserves.

If introversion is part of the picture, working with energy-rebound strategies becomes essential. These clients need to replenish energy expended on social exchanges. Recharge times can be short breaks during the day or longer breaks in their weekly schedule. The key is that the recharge does not involve social interaction and is a diversion from daily work activities. For example:

- Meditating—a recharge on all levels: spiritual, emotional, and physical
- Working out—especially alone as in running or swimming
- Reading or listening to music
- Gardening or walking in nature

THERAPEUTIC RELATIONSHIP

Panicky and depressed clients are looking for clear guidance on how to minimize their panic symptoms and do not always recognize how much depression interferes with their progress. They want direction, but at times they feel the therapist's expectations might be too high. A positive alliance can develop quickly if the therapist takes time to support therapeutic suggestions with education about why the methods are likely to work. Support and encouragement are always factors in developing a therapeutic alliance, but they are most important for the panicky, depressed client.

ADDRESSING THE SYMPTOMS

It is usually possible to initiate symptom management very early in treatment. Panicky and depressed clients are eager to get control over their panic. When depression is mild, they can typically muster enough mental and physical energy to make lifestyle changes and use panic management techniques.

Lifestyle

Because these clients' depression is usually only mild or moderate, lifestyle issues such as exercise are typically not especially problematic. Making any physical health adjustments that may be necessary and putting energy-rebound strategies into place are the first order of business.

Education About Panic Attacks

It is quite common for panicky clients to come to therapy already on medication, typically an SSRI and often with a benzodiazepine. This can present a therapy problem, as clients may believe their panic and depression are going to be hard to get rid of because medication has not worked. In these cases, educating clients about panic attacks is crucial.

Specific Therapy Tools for Change

There is a case to be made for simply learning that physical panic symptoms are without intrinsic meaning, can be tolerated and will pass, and therefore only need to be "ridden out" by the client. Several styles of therapy take this valid approach. However, many of my clients want to know they can do something about their panic, and, in fact, there are things that clients can do to manage arousal effectively.

Predict, Prepare, and Plan for Panic

The key to treating panic is reducing its frequency, duration, and intensity. From a brain-based point of view, the less you panic, the less you will panic. Frequent or intense panic attacks sensitize the brain, making it easier for a new attack to occur. A diminishment of attacks reverses that sensitivity, as does desensitizing known triggers. Panicky, depressed clients feel more empowered when they know they have tools to handle panic.

Predict, Prepare, and Plan helps them get those tools. First, clients are asked to predict what situations might trigger a panic attack. The goal of identifying these situations is not to encourage avoidance of them but rather to pave the way for the preparing and planning steps.

Next, clients prepare for how they will be in the situation without panicking. The specific therapy tools outlined on the following pages can be used during this stage of the process.

Finally, clients plan for what to do if a panic attack actually does occur. Certain strategies for preventing an attack, such as diaphragmatic breathing, can also be used to stop one that's already begun, but clients may also want to make additional plans. For example, if a client is afraid of having a panic attack while in a meeting, she might plan to have a peppermint to pop in her mouth, which provides an immediate sensory shift to distract her from panic "warning" signs. Or she could plan what to say to excuse herself if she feels she would do better to leave the room for a moment.

It's worth noting here that many therapists advocate treatment that encourages acceptance of symptoms as neutral sensations (what they call "floating with panic"). The idea is that these interoceptive exposure experiences will help clients practice acceptance and change cognitive attitudes toward panic. Although this approach does work with many clients, I have found that clients with panic and depression are often somewhat passive, and I want to bolster their sense of competence and control by encouraging them to take charge of their feelings and behaviors. Predict, Prepare, and Plan is an empowering strategy that works to counteract the helpless feelings of depression.

Diaphragmatic Breathing

Diaphragmatic breathing can be used to avert a panic attack before it's begun, and it is the one technique that will slow and stop panic once it is underway. This is because breathing, especially with a long exhalation, initiates activity in the parasympathetic nervous system, helping to reduce heart rate, tension, and other symptoms produced by the sympathetic nervous system. Because breath can be controlled by an act of will, clients can take charge of panic even when they feel out of control otherwise.

Breathing needs to be practiced (this can be part of a recharge plan, too). Once a day, clients take time to build the duration of breathing up to at least 5 minutes (the amount needed to quell a panic attack that has started). These practice sessions can be done at home or even at work as a mini-break. Clients can use apps downloaded to their smartphone or computer that both remind them to breathe and time their practice session.

Panic Diary

The Panic Diary is used to help clients identify the places and situations in which they have panicked. On an index card or in their handheld device, clients record the following notes about the attack:

- What time it was
- How long the panic lasted
- The location
- The severity of the attack
- What happened just before the attack started

Whereas the first items in the list simply help a client be more of an observer and less a victim, what happened just before the attack is the important thing to monitor.

In Shannon's case it seemed obvious: If someone started discussing suicide, she would feel panic arise. But to her surprise, when we examined the exact trigger, it was actually her inner statement—"This could have been my fault!"—that set the panic in motion.

Once they have identified situations (or thoughts) that could trigger a panic attack, clients can predict panic and go into those situations ready to handle them. They also need to plan for what to do if they *do* happen to panic. This planning involves detailed, step-by-step actions.

Shannon planned to do diaphragmatic breathing if she felt panic coming on while she was in the teachers' lounge. If that didn't seem to be working quickly enough, she would politely excuse herself and enter the restroom to run cool water over her hands while breathing and doing some calming self-talk.

The more Shannon could be in the lounge, the more she would realize that suicide was not the sole topic of conversation, and this would help her begin to relax. Because we had also identified that she was introverted, Shannon chose not to go to the lounge when she felt exhausted or had experienced too many draining interactions with others during the day.

What Hurts to Think About?

This technique is used specifically with clients who complain of headaches. It worked extremely well with Shannon.

When we began tracking Shannon's migraines, we discovered that they were interesting in their origin. There was a clear stress onset, but I wondered about the exact type of stress, so I asked Shannon (first in sessions when her head hurt and later over the phone when she called to tell me a migraine had set in), "What hurts to think about?" This question never failed to reveal a problem of plunging self-esteem provoked by a criticism or a fear of failure in a particular situation. Identifying the problem she did not want to think about frequently alleviated the migraine. At first I helped her do this by asking the question when she called me, but as time went on she learned to ask herself.

"What Did I Do?"

When depressed clients develop panic, and the panic is not attached to a specific situation, they attempt to find an explanation for the panic so that it won't feel so frighteningly unpredictable or unexplainable. People seem to feel less frightened of things they can explain. As I mentioned earlier, the guilt underlying a client's panic may stem from an imagined wrongdoing or from a real one. Let's look at guilt for imagined wrongdoing first. I call this "potential guilt": "I might have done something wrong, and I'm not sure I did, but if I did, I would feel very bad about it."

Potential guilt is feeling guilty because something you've done *may have* resulted in negative outcomes for someone. For example, a person may start to feel guilty about making an offhand remark that might have offended someone (such as commenting about people who "take advantage of the government for welfare" and later realizing a person in the conversation had once used food stamps when unemployed). The client wonders if that person was hurt and feels guilty about making the remark, but cannot go back and check whether the remark was taken personally without creating a worse situation. This leads clients to ruminate about their possible wrongdoing and exacerbates the anxiety they were trying to explain to themselves.

The "What Did I Do?" technique works well in these cases. Clients are encouraged to ask this question. Remember that this kind of worry is an unplanned attempt to get rid of anxiety by a) identifying possible guilt as a reason for feeling bad, and then b) talking to themselves about why it is not so bad. But worrying makes anxiety worse; the nature of potential guilt is such that clients can never ascertain whether or not they should feel bad. Clarifying that there is no use in thinking about a situation that cannot be resolved will help them to acknowledge that there is no clear reason to feel bad. They feel bad because they are in a state of anxiety, not because they have done something wrong. Then, if they slip back into ruminating about potential guilt, they are instructed to immediately apply Thought-Stopping and Thought-Replacing (see Chapter 9) to avoid or minimize panic.

In other cases, clients actually do have a credible answer to the question "What did I do?" People with addiction in their history will have guilt about how they treated their bodies, how they spent money, how they handled relationships, and so on. Clients who have had an affair, have been at fault in an accident, or have acted rashly in the heat of the moment may ruminate incessantly on these mistakes they regret making. When depression is added into the mix, these clients have a hard time mentally walking away or permanently dismissing their worries. And whenever they find themselves in a situation in which they might again make such a mistake, panic hits.

Resolution can be achieved in these cases by following these four simple steps:

1. First, clients identify their actions, writing down what they actually did without self-blame or explanation as part of the description.

2. The next step is for clients to acknowledge to a safe person (usually the therapist) that they have some responsibility for the actions.

3. Together with that safe person, clients then decide what it would take to make restitution.

4. Finally, clients make restitution if a direct action is possible. If direct action toward repairing the situation isn't possible, clients can make what 12-step programs call "living amends," which means changing the way they live from that day forward in a manner that recognizes and affirms what was learned from the error. For example, if a client had an affair, he or she could commit to a life of honesty and faithfulness from that day forward.

Although Roger's outburst at work wasn't an egregious mistake, he nevertheless worried about whether it would happen again. He assumed devastating consequences would follow if it did, which kept his tension high. In answering the question "What did I do?" Roger identified that he made a rash statement when feeling pressed and frustrated. This was a mistake that he needed to forgive himself for. In this case, there was no restitution needed, except maybe to assure his spouse that he would not be rash in that way again. However, we did need to work on self-compassion, and part of that was understanding what had led to his outburst.

Change Your Thinking About Panic

Managing panic is easier if clients can change their thinking about having panic. Many people who suffer from panic have beliefs about the power of panic that make the experience of having it even worse. These beliefs tend to be even more embedded when clients also suffer from the feelings of helplessness that accompany depression. If those beliefs can be altered, the client's relationship to panic changes.

When people have a panic attack, they feel like they are dying. This feeling is so strong that the person dreads ever having another attack. But nobody actually dies from having a panic attack. Therefore, the first cognition to focus on is: *Panic is unpleasant but not lethal.* And then: *I can tolerate panic attacks when they occur, and life—even a pleasant life—will go on.*

Another cognition that is helpful has to do the sensation of needing to flee when feeling panic. *I can panic and stay right where I am. It will pass.* People can pretty much do whatever they want while having a panic attack as long as they focus on what they are doing and on letting the sensations pass. Of course, panic is distracting, so it might be unwise to drive or "operate heavy machinery," but you *can* be around others while you wait it out.

Stop Catastrophizing

Panicky clients with depression readily see the negatives of life and consequently find it easy to believe that the outcome of their panic will be catastrophic. Usually the catastrophe involves dying, going crazy, or losing control of oneself. Listen to what these clients fear, discuss the likelihood of those feared outcomes actually occurring, and then find corrective statements that clients can substitute.

> *Roger's primary catastrophic thoughts were related to the first time he panicked and ended up losing his job. His primary fear was: "If I panic, I will lose control and say something that will get me fired again." He also had the persistent belief that he would "never get over this." (That was his depression speaking.) He challenged these beliefs by reminding himself that he now had a plan to relieve his frustration before he got to the point of blurting out. He also developed other*

new, less catastrophic thoughts: "Even if I panic, I can keep control of what I say aloud," and "Even if others see me panic, I can deal with the embarrassment I might feel."

Small Steps and a Well-Controlled Exit Strategy

Clients' thoughts affect their feelings and behaviors. When they think panic makes change impossible, those thoughts will block them from creating a life less dominated by fear.

When they are ready to make a plan about how to live without fear, ask clients what specific changes they think will lead to a more contented life. Small steps toward change that can be reasonably accomplished are crucial: The more realistic those small steps are, the more likely the client will be to accomplish them. And the more successful clients are in making changes, the more likely they will be to have faith that more change can happen. This is especially the case when clients are changing in a new direction rather than returning to a level of functioning they previously were capable of. For example, a person who was very relaxed at work before receiving a terrible evaluation may be able to get back to his pre-evaluation relaxation without enormous difficulty. But suppose that person *never* trusted his judgment at work? Bringing him to the point of feeling competent will be much slower because the behaviors will all be new.

A well-controlled exit strategy is also important. Part of the dread about having a panic attack has to do with worries about making a fool of oneself in front of other people. As mentioned earlier, clients should be reminded that they don't have to flee whatever situation they are in if they begin to panic, but in some cases removing oneself from the situation is necessary. Help clients develop a plan to gracefully exit new situations without creating embarrassment.

Shannon feared her colleagues judged her as being standoffish or unfriendly, which she was not. She just didn't have the energy to deal with students all day and also interact with colleagues. But she also knew that daily school life would be easier if she had friendly relationships, and she knew she felt more cheerful when she had pleasant social conversation with fellow teachers. Once she got her panic under better control, she decided that improving collegial relationships would be a good target to help her feel less depression.

Keeping in mind her limited energy, Shannon thought eating lunch in the lounge would be a good choice. She could bring her own food, arrive when it suited her, and leave when she wanted. She started with 15 minutes—about half of her allotted lunch time—to stop in the lounge with her sandwich and chat with colleagues. Her exit plan was to say that she needed to catch up on some work and excuse herself. Shannon quickly found that the others welcomed her and did not react negatively if she excused herself. This made it easier to go on a daily basis and she did not feel too drained from the contact.

ONGOING THERAPY

As therapy for panic proceeds, the depression may prove to interfere with progress or at certain points command more attention than the panic attacks. Typically the tendency toward self-criticism flares and is more obvious when panic is not the automatic outcome. Because in depression people scan the world for negativity, opportunities to judge oneself are not hard to find. These judgments can relate to any aspect of life: at work, at school, in hobbies, in athletics, as homemakers, or as parents, partners, or friends—you name it, depressed people can feel bad about it. The major goal here is to stop any reaction to situations before evaluating whether the negative self-appraisal is warranted. Rooting out the tendency to blame oneself often involves putting in a time delay before assigning blame in order to isolate the negative thought and correct it.

Find the Trigger, Delay the Action

Once clients begin to see the process they go through, they can delay action, including negative self-appraisals, until they have evaluated the situation more clearly.

> Shannon did very well with getting rid of her feeling of potential guilt, and her panic diminished markedly. But although she was functioning better in all respects, she still tended to be very self-critical. And that was the biggest underlying cause of her depression (and her migraines).
>
> Shannon's history included a difficult relationship with her mother, who was judgmental and often criticized her. As we did insight-oriented work on their relationship, Shannon began to recognize that her migraines were a clue that her self-criticism was activated. With that in mind, she began stopping to evaluate what self-criticism had come up whenever she felt a headache developing. Typically, she could hear her mother's voice. She worked on this over several months by stopping to explore what the criticism was and whether it was valid (usually not!), and then replacing the negative statement with a more positive and realistic self-appraisal. For example, if she thought she should have been friendlier to a peer, instead of hearing her mother's voice telling her she never behaved correctly in social situations, she told herself that her friends know she is quiet and would not take it personally. This process netted excellent results in identifying and fending off depressed feelings.

Restore Pleasurable Activities

When clients are panicky and depressed, they tend to pull back from activities that at one time were pleasurable or restorative for them. Adding these activities back in, once clients are not excessively concerned about panicking, helps to reverse the depression. You may need to do some digging if it has been some time since they were regularly doing activities that were pleasurable, but if the depression is mild or moderate, chances are good that they will be able to gradually restore some degree of pleasing activity. As they do, it will become easier to do more, and eventually they will achieve better balance in their wellbeing.

> *As he panicked less, practicing breathing reminded Roger of when he used to meditate. He spontaneously added a meditation class into his week, which he found immensely helpful. He loved the principles underlying the practice, and the ability to connect with others through a shared experience of silence suited his introversion. Learning mindfulness, both through classes and by studying online, aided his recovery from depression.*

FINISHING UP

Because panic tends to return when clients are under stress, planning relapse management is important. If they have even one panic attack, clients often will feel as if their whole problem is back. Three steps help with planning to prevent or deal with a relapse.

- *Predict panic!* Help clients make a plan for what to do if they have a panic attack. Part of this involves planning not to panic about having the attack!

- *Build resilience.* Resilience helps clients deal with stress. Exercise, positive relationships with others, spiritual development, and good physical self-care are among the things that build resilience.
- *Establish pleasurable activities.* Well-established pleasurable activities will bring balance into clients' lives.

> *Shannon found that boosting her exercise regime was incredibly healing. She began training to run marathons and was ready for her first marathon when she completed therapy. The long runs perfectly suited her need to be alone and to discharge energy.*
>
> *Roger began to study philosophy of religions, and this, along with his meditation, matched his desire to quietly embrace the spiritual and philosophical interests he had stopped pursuing earlier in his life.*

TREATMENT SUMMARY FOR THE PANICKY AND DEPRESSED CLIENT

Assessment

Physical health—no common health problems underlie this condition, but evaluate intake of stimulating substances or medications as well as hormone status for women

- Readiness to change—typically the client is motivated and ready to work in treatment
- Mental energy—the mild or moderate depression does not interfere with the ability to learn panic management skills;

however, panic may increase depression, resulting in lower mental energy

Introversion

Introverted clients may be more susceptible to withdrawing from peers, especially if their panic occurs in social contexts. Identify specific ways the client can recharge throughout a day and after expending social energy.

Therapeutic Relationship

Therapeutic alliance usually develops quickly and can be fostered with optimism and information about how panic management methods will work.

Addressing the Symptoms

There are no common lifestyle issues to address here, except if the client is a woman with hormonal issues triggering panic.

Education About Panic Attacks

Clients feel more optimistic about recovery and comply better with treatment suggestions when they know how panic is triggered and how the techniques diminish physical symptoms and emotional distress.

Specific Therapy Tools for Change
- Predict, Prepare, and Plan for Panic
- Diaphragmatic breathing
- Panic Diary
- What Hurts to Think About?

- "What Did I Do?" (to distinguish potential guilt from real guilt and determine how to respond to guilty feelings)
- Change Your Thinking About Panic ("panic isn't lethal"; "I can tolerate panic"; "the panic will pass")
- Stop Catastrophizing (about both having symptoms and the outcome of symptoms)
- Small Steps and a Well-Controlled Exit Strategy

Ongoing Therapy
- Find the Trigger, Delay the Action
- Restore Pleasurable Activities

Finishing Up
- Predict panic and educate about relapse
- Build resilience
- Establish pleasurable activities

CHAPTER 6

THE WORRIED & EXHAUSTED CLIENT

The worried and exhausted client is keeping up with daily living requirements but is becoming increasingly fearful of failing to perform in the future. Feeling stressed and overtaxed, these clients tend to be low on energy for therapy. The following checklist indicates the main characteristics of worried and exhausted clients.

|||||||||||||||||||||||||||||||||||||||||||||||||||||||||||||||||||||||

_____ *"Stressed out" emotional and physical state.* The client describes him- or herself as being "stressed out."

_____ *Persistent, ruminative worry.* This worry tends to focus on potential problems rather than actual ones. The client finds this ruminative worry distressing.

_____ *Ability to manage real and immediate problems without worry.* Many anxious clients find this confusing, because they can see that when they are presented with an actual problem (rather than a feared one) they are often able to deal with it without becoming consumed by worry.

_____ *Insufficient or nonrestorative sleep.* The client may be sleeping too little or may fail to feel refreshed even by a normal amount of sleep.

_____ *Exhaustion.* This is a complaint but is not the reason the client seeks therapy.

_____ *Extensive efforts to solve problems.* Highly responsible in general, the client increases work to solve problems, which worsens exhaustion.

_____ *Rigid approaches to problem-solving.* The client feels "stuck" in thinking and action.

_____ *Poor problem-solving for anxiety and depression.* Although he or she is often a good troubleshooter, the client has difficulty managing his or her own symptoms of anxiety and depression.

_____ *Blindness to the severity of the situation.* The client is often unwilling to take new action or change patterns because he or she doesn't see the problem as being as extreme as it actually is.

_____ *Lack of tenacity in efforts to change.* The client may quickly give up if he or she hits roadblocks in changing patterns and habits.

||||||||||||||||||||||||||||||||||||||||||||||||||||||||||||||||||||||||||||

I see this client as having a combination of generalized anxiety and dysphoric depression consequent to exhaustion. The worried and exhausted client is usually someone who is burned out or on the way to burnout. People with this combination of anxiety and depression probably experienced anxiety first, and that anxiety fueled a "make no mistakes" approach to life. The worry eventually becomes debilitating and interferes with solving problems. These clients tend to be highly responsible people but are cognitively rigid in their problem-solving styles—a common condition among people with generalized anxiety.

By the time they enter treatment, these clients are exhausted by their own worrying. At that point it may be unclear whether depression is fueling the exhaustion or vice versa. What *is* clear is that the interrelationship between their worrying and their chronically stressful life situation resulted in the depression and exhaustion.

Therapy in these cases must, at the outset of treatment, tackle lifestyle changes, stress management, and cognitive shifts about the client's sense of personal responsibility. Often, however, these clients are not able or willing to make lifestyle or behavioral changes quickly. Therefore, therapy must begin by focusing on cognitive change—getting the client to agree that something has to give.

A CASE OF THE WORRIED AND EXHAUSTED CLIENT

Celia, 48, was a classic worrier. She was employed as a manager to troubleshoot franchise startups, a job she was so good at that she frequently received recruitment phone calls from other companies wishing to hire her. Her most recent post was a very stressful job she had taken because it allowed her to live near her mother, who had recently entered a nursing facility.

Celia had worked in several locations around the country and had made and kept friends from every place she worked. However, she had no close friends in the city she was now living in, and she felt sad and lonely. She was not romantically involved with anyone.

"Frankly," she said, "who has time for romance anymore? I barely have time to shop for a new pair of shoes."

Celia stopped in to visit her mother almost daily to "keep tabs on" the situation and be sure her mother was well cared for. She was also trying to straighten out her mother's finances, which were a mess. However, she needed information from her mother to do this, and her mother was showing worsening memory problems. According to Celia, there was no escape from this escalating burden of responsibility. "At this point," she said, "I need way more than a vacation."

Arnie presented a different example of the worried and exhausted client.

Arnie, 60, was not naturally gregarious, and some of his isolation felt comforting and restorative to him. He said he had been "nervous all my life," but that he "went over the edge" when his brother was diagnosed with pancreatic cancer. Arnie immediately dropped everything to help out, taking on responsibility for maintenance of his brother's home and yard, running errands for his brother's wife, and doing whatever else he could to make their lives easier. At first this made him feel helpful, but as his brother's condition worsened, Arnie began to realize that his efforts would not save his brother, and he felt more and more like a failure. Arnie's worries soon escalated to include worry about his sister-in-law, about his own health and susceptibility to cancer, and about how long his brother would live and how he would feel when his brother died. He attempted to handle his worry by working harder, but this exhausted him even further, which made his worrying worse. Naturally a man who needed alone time, Arnie was busy every moment with his brother and sister-in-law. "My worrying is driving me crazy!" he declared.

ASSESSMENT

When clients have stressful lives that intensify anxiety and worry, paying attention to their health will always be part of the treatment picture, because health problems are a frequent consequence of burnout.

Physical Health

The most common physical condition underlying the worried and exhausted client's condition is burnout. Burnout leads to health issues more often than it is caused by them. First and foremost, looking at sleep is a must. Sleeping fitfully is frequently related to worrying rather than to parasomnias like sleep apnea. Additionally, these clients may not be sleeping enough hours because of their nonstop activity.

Nutrition is also a concern, because under chronic stress people tend not to do a good job of cooking or taking time for appropriate meals.

Finally, chronic stress will worsen all tension-related illness, and health problems like autoimmune disorders, blood pressure problems, or heart disease can either exacerbate or be exacerbated by stress.

> *Celia was not in good shape. She was on medication for high blood pressure, which she suspected had been caused by the combination of her recent weight gain and the stress of her job and the situation with her mother. She had a physical when she took her new job, and all her other numbers were in the high normal range. "I guess I better start paying attention, huh?" was her response to how she felt when she got that information. She knew she needed to diet and exercise but she saw no way to make those two things happen as long*

as she was overseeing the care of her mother, whose needs dominated her time. She was inflexible on this point.

Readiness to Change

Burnout is complicated by denial: As people progress down the path of working harder to get control of a situation or become more involved in caring for others, they lose the capacity to see the reality of their situation. They will tell you they are perfectly willing and able to stop the working or caretaking as soon as the situation changes. They believe that "if I just work a little harder, I will get the work done and then I will take care of myself," but they fail to see that the work will not ever be done or not be done soon enough. As these worrying, highly responsible people take on increasing levels of responsibility, they continue to deny the fact that it's causing them stress. Their inner dialogue is something like: "I'll just get through this and then I will relax." But such time for relaxation never comes. They also will completely agree that stress is a problem in our society, but they have no insight into the damage it may be causing them personally. So, although they are ready to change on the one hand, their denial blocks substantial movement to a healthier lifestyle that could lighten worry and exhaustion.

The burnout makes their mental rigidity harder to deal with. Being cognitively stuck is a hallmark feature of the worried and exhausted client, and it interferes with readiness to change. These clients become unable to see any alternatives to their situations, although they express a desire to figure something else out. The exhaustion also limits their ability to manage worry, and their mental rigidity interferes with changing cognitions. Starting out therapy with suggestions for change will garner defensiveness, so attention needs to first go to developing awareness of the trouble they are in.

Education about burnout is key to moving clients from theoretical readiness to genuine readiness.

> *At least one part of Celia thought, "I can handle it. This exhaustion and anxiety are not as big a deal as I am making them out to be." She was not ready for the stage of taking action because her anxiety was made worse by her mental inflexibility—she was mentally and behaviorally stuck. She needed to learn what burnout is and identify her stage of burnout. I recommended a book on this topic and we discussed it as a way to begin challenging her thoughts on burnout.*

Mental Energy

If the client is still able to maintain work-related functioning, he or she probably has the mental energy necessary to do therapy. Although they are tired, these clients are not necessarily passive. If they are worried and stress exhausts them, pay attention to whether you see burnout behavior: working more or longer hours, or not taking breaks from caretaking.

But burnout doesn't underlie the exhaustion of all clients. Some clients may be more passive or suffer from a generalized anxiety disorder that so consumes their mental energy that they stop functioning efficiently in their lives. These clients may lack the resilience and coping skills necessary for facing stressful life circumstances. When this is the case, I investigate with clients not only how they cope with stress but also the ways they have been affected by stress in the past. If clients do not appear to be resilient, part of the therapy will focus on getting through the current challenge and then improving resilience with both lifestyle and cognitive changes.

Arnie needed to improve his resilience. His worrying started easily and he was completely overwhelmed by it. When stressful life circumstances occurred, he did not have strong resources ready to deal with them. His overall attitude was passive—he didn't believe he could affect life's circumstances. He did not have a lot of friends to offer support, he had not developed a spiritual life that could comfort him or bring him hope, and he was not a man who would join a support group. He often felt—and was—alone. Although he was willing to accept suggestions from therapy, he was not filled with optimism about his ability to change.

Another consideration in mental energy is the mental inflexibility that is the hallmark of a worrying brain. It takes a lot of energy to fight against worry, but switching gears or generating new solutions also takes energy. People who are intensely worried generally have difficulty problem-solving for their own situations. These clients may show little ability to find new thoughts or ideas for themselves despite being good troubleshooters for others.

Celia was exhausted, but she was okay with regard to mental energy. She was perhaps stuck, but she was also willing to think things through. She was not a passive person, so if therapy could help her with the denial of burnout, she would make good progress with mental and behavioral change. She believed in her ability to handle life and saw this time as an anomaly in her usual pattern of worrying but functioning well.

THERAPEUTIC RELATIONSHIP

Worried and exhausted clients often have started out as highly productive, and they do not want to feel that others, including the therapist, somehow manage life better than they do. But they do want a collaborative relationship with a therapist who serves as a resource and whose goals are in line with their own. These clients want and benefit from receiving empathy for the position in which they find themselves. They are very sensitive to being told what they need to do, and they will tend to feel judged when they are given ideas that are counter to the ways they have been trying to solve their problems.

A helpful therapeutic beginning is starting with unconditional support for the problems they experience and using their own words to describe their situation. This creates an extremely collaborative relationship that can break through denial about the problems caused by current burnout behavior, and goals can be set while avoiding concerns about judgment.

Celia had a lot of wisdom, even though exhaustion prevented access to that wisdom. She believed she chose correctly in taking the new job and caring for her mother. She saw no other way to do this. She needed time to understand how burnout interfered with her thinking and limited her range of options. Then she would become better able to make her own decisions and value the therapeutic support.

Arnie needed empathy but he more urgently wanted to stop worrying now. He was receptive to getting new ideas and saw my encouragement to try them as being supportive.

ADDRESSING THE SYMPTOMS

When people are burned out, it is usually necessary to start with lifestyle issues. Worried and exhausted clients want to dig in to solve the problems they worry about, but one of the biggest concerns is addressing their exhaustion so they have energy to do therapy.

Lifestyle

This is the place for obvious changes, good sleep hygiene coming first. (If you aren't sure how to help people sleep better, visit the website of the American Academy of Sleep Medicine at www. aasmnet.org, which is loaded with ideas for promoting restful sleep.) But it's also important to look at the client's eating habits, nutrition, and follow-through on medical issues. Worried and exhausted clients will be all over the map on these issues, from overeating to undereating, sitting on the couch to overexercising, ignoring healthcare to overusing medical resources. With women, always check whether stage-of-life hormone-related concerns may be contributing to their situation.

> *Lifestyle changes were a big challenge for Celia, who needed to take care of herself nutritionally and physically. Continuously working at her job and on her mother's finances had started her down a path to ill health with weight gain and high blood pressure.*

Specific Therapy Tools for Change

Worried and exhausted clients need to start slowly because their energy is very limited. It is also important to pay attention to the things that are most in line with the client's degree of willingness to change. Remember that clients' denial might prevent recognition of the importance of change, but feeling permission to shift a little at a time can make it possible for them to improve. This is what the first technique in this section is about.

The next two techniques address burnout. Once clients are trapped in the burnout cycle, it can be hard to escape. The client works hard to solve problems, which leads to exhaustion, and in an effort to end the exhaustion, the client works harder to solve the problems, which only increases the exhaustion. Denial underlies this whole cycle—clients simply refuse to see the deleterious effects of their overwork, clinging to the belief that once they just "fix these few things," everything will be solved. Breaking into this denial is crucial, and the first step is education on burnout. After that, the two-part technique "What Are My Values?" and What Is the Dichotomy? can be used. If the worried and exhausted client is not burned out, examining the impact of worry and exhaustion on quality of life is important. This technique will increase motivation, improve cooperation, and foster insight about the reality of their situation.

Finally, cognitive errors must be addressed. Worried and exhausted clients entertain a whole host of cognitive errors, including that they have no choice in the situation (i.e., that there is no other way to handle it), that they alone are responsible for solving the problematic situation, and that it is their "duty" to worry about the situation (and they must worry about it *all the time*). Three techniques help challenge these beliefs: There Is Always a Choice; "Am I, and Only I, Responsible for This?"; and Contain Worry in Time.

The last two techniques presented in this section—Change Behavior, Change Cognitions, and Ask for Help, Allow for Help— focus on changing problematic behavioral patterns.

Do What You Think Is Best on This List

As a way to begin the collaboration and join with clients' own wisdom about what they need, suggest that your clients compose a list of things they believe could help with their exhaustion. As you go through the list, you will be able to see if they are thinking clearly about their needs or if they need input about where to start. Be sure they have considered nutrition, sleep, and time outside as part of their relaxation and exercise plan. Then ask them to do whatever they think is best as a place to start, emphasizing that they aren't expected to do everything on the list immediately. Check with them occasionally, but not every session, about their progress on accomplishing the goal they chose.

> *Celia's list included daily exercise, cooking at home instead of eating fast food, and taking time to relax. I asked if she could add a few simple, specific things to her list: take a multivitamin daily, walk the dog for a few minutes instead of just letting him out in the yard, take a few extra minutes each day to spend in the shower relaxing, and allowing herself 10 minutes of alone time to work a puzzle or read a novel. I told her we could come back to this from time to time to see what she was doing.*

Education on Burnout

Education about burnout helps the client realize that changing patterns may be necessary. Educating can include talking about how burnout begins with normal caring actions and persists even in the face of clear self-harm, as well as looking at progression charts or reading books on burnout. (See the resource section on assessments for Freudenberger and North, Women's Burnout, which can be informative about men as well, Neff on Self-Compassion (and take her test online!), or look at the research of Arie Shirom and his team.)

"What Are My Values?"

In order to make changes in their daily lives, worried and exhausted clients need to examine the reasons they do things and look at how decisions were originally made. Denial is often kept in place by unexamined values and lack of awareness regarding how values undergird choices.

Many people never articulate what values they uphold with their words and behavior, and opening a discussion about values can gently break clients' denial about the negative impact of their over-work. One way to begin this discussion is to use a chart to identify various values and list the ways the client lives them out.

For example, one of my clients, an associate partner in a prestigious law firm, was a divorced father of two young children. The custody arrangement stipulated that the children spend weekends with him and weekdays with their mother. One of this client's values was to be "the perfect father," and he upheld this value by spending time with his children even when his work demanded overtime. Another value was "being promoted to partner," and he upheld this by pulling all-nighters on weekends, spending the day with his children and nights working from home.

Identifying these values should be done in writing so the client can more easily prioritize them, which is the next step.

What Is the Dichotomy?

The first step in this part of the technique is prioritizing values. This can be difficult when simultaneously upholding two different values is impossible. For example, although the client I just mentioned valued being a good father and advancing at his firm, he couldn't fulfill both as well as he wanted to: The time he spent with his children cut into the overtime he needed to do to get promoted to partner, and the all-nighters he was pulling to get work done made him irritable and short-tempered with his kids during the day, in addition to affecting his work performance.

Identifying dichotomies like this is the crux of this technique, and understanding the impact of unspoken priorities helps break clients' denial about their exhaustion and encourages them to make changes in their lifestyle. One way to do this is by putting two opposing views or actions side by side in a "I would rather _____ than _____" format, or by uniting two opposing ideas with the word *and*. Placing these values side by side is typically a surprising experience for clients. For example: "I would rather get promoted to partner than spend a lot of time with my children." This statement caused him some discomfort because he did not actually agree with it, but it helped him acknowledge that his choice to prioritize work on weekends was negatively affecting his parenting. Or, "I want to spend my weekend time with my children and I want to spend my weekend time on my law practice." That statement revealed the tension of his actual decision in a way that prompted discussion instead of continuing to attempt to do both.

Once their values are prioritized, you can further discuss whether clients want to maintain them as priorities and whether there may be other ways to uphold them. For example, after several sessions of discussion, the client trying to make partner decided that work needed to be his main priority at least until he was promoted. After brainstorming about other ways to uphold his value of being a good father, he decided to invite his mother to spend weekends with them—an idea that pleased her because it gave her more time to see her grandchildren, and that allowed him to get work done while she prepared meals and put the kids to bed.

Celia similarly needed to examine her values and beliefs. Some of those values and beliefs were ill-considered, and some contradicted other values. For example, she believed it was her duty to care for her mother, and she also believed she should take good care of herself. Those two values couldn't both be upheld in the way she was carrying them out. I worked with Celia to find exactly the right words to describe her dilemma, and we came up with: "I would rather never

fulfill my own goals and would even die trying to take care of my
mother's needs than not take care of my mother and deal with her
criticism and guilt-inducing comments." I asked Celia to write this
down on an index card and read it aloud a couple of times. After
she spoke these words, she asked, "Now what?" I told her she should
simply read the sentence and let it sit. Feeling the conflict and its
negative impact might eventually motivate her to initiate changes
she could live with.

There Is Always a Choice

The inability to perceive choice is a common theme among people
with cognitive rigidity and inflexibility in problem-solving. One
common powerful cognition among worried and exhausted clients
has to do with their inability to handle cognitive "stuckness." They
say to themselves, "I have no choice." They see no way out of their
situation, and no alternative ways to handle it: "I must work at this
job, keep this house I hate, continue doing things the way I currently do them." Of course, seeing oneself as stuck means not having to make an effort to change.

First, clients need to acknowledge that choices exist.

> *Celia was extremely concerned about the cost of her mother's*
> *healthcare. Her mother's health was worsening, and higher levels of*
> *care would cost more than what her mother had prepared for finan-*
> *cially. Celia's image of publicly funded nursing facilities stopped her*
> *from thinking about them as an option. "There's no way I'm sending*
> *her to one of those places," she adamantly stated. "Briarwood is the*
> *only place around here with a good reputation." Her focus on that one*
> *healthcare center prevented her from understanding what the choices*
> *might be.*

One useful technique in this situation is Worry Well and Only Once. As described in Chapter 3, this technique entails identifying all the potential glitches, problems, and resources that need to be filled. Then all the information is gathered, plans to gain access to resources are made, and worrying is declared done.

> *Celia agreed to worry well and only once. She would consult a specialist in senior care to find a good solution. She would also identify markers of her mother's behavior that might indicate a need to review the situation at the more affordable facility.*

"Am I, and Only I, Responsible for This?"

With worried and exhausted clients, it is often necessary to address the element of personal responsibility. In their own way, they each say, "I, and only I, am responsible for this." Remember that people with extreme worry tend to be poor problem-solvers when it comes to their own anxiety and its causes, and when worriers are also exhausted, they lack the energy to see their situation differently. Simply and gently challenging their belief that they alone are responsible can be like a healthy splash of cold water to wake them up.

> *Arnie was adamant: He must do all he could for his brother because there was not much time left to do it. However, the big issue—"I cannot save him"—played into this belief. If Arnie could see that feelings of responsibility were a sort of false reality and that he was not in fact responsible for his brother's illness or recovery but only for caring about him, he might worry less, I thought. As Arnie had declared that his worry was driving him crazy, we started there. I also knew his worry was interfering with sleep, so I suggested that he try containing his worry in time, the next technique.*

Contain Worry in Time

This method addresses the issue of responsibility by acknowledging there may be nothing to actually do—even in serious situations that cannot be easily dismissed. Clients often have a mistaken cognition that they must worry. When this is the case, we can encourage clients to worry their hearts out, but to confine that worry to a limited 10-minute period each day, preferably at the same time of day. (When people have trouble sleeping, it is possible to do this right before sleep to send the brain the message "You are done for the night!") Clients use the worry time to pour all their worries about a specific situation into that period, setting a timer so they don't watch the clock (and because the brain is prepared to turn off when it hears a "ding" signaling "done."). Clients who use visualization well can consider lighting a candle and visualizing the light streaming from the candle into the world, where it surrounds the person they are worrying about with love and protection from pain, fear, loss, and so on. When the timer dings, clients tell themselves, "I am done for today." If the worries reemerge after the worry time is done, clients remind themselves, "I will worry about all of this again tomorrow."

Change Behavior, Change Cognitions

Actually making behavioral change is vital to breaking the rigid thinking that is a hallmark of worried and exhausted clients. In therapy, these clients need to discuss specific situations they feel stuck in so that you can help them find small steps toward getting "unstuck" that they are willing to undertake. These small steps often involve the client's asking another person to help with some part of a work project, a family situation, or a volunteer task.

Ask for Help, Allow for Help

Asking people for help can be hard for these clients, but actually allowing them to help can be even harder. Remind clients to practice "good manners": When other people volunteer to do a part of the task, clients should thank them and let them do it. Clients should not micromanage the volunteer's help or offer to pitch in with the work. For example, suppose a client's friend volunteers to drop off a book your client wants. The client should not suggest that they meet halfway or offer to pick up the book himself. Remember, your burned out clients got that way by doing things without help; they don't want others to work on their behalf in case the other will overreach, get tired, or resent them. They have little practice in letting others pitch in to do work, and rarely notice that other people may even like to be helpful.

> *Celia needed to address her over-responsibility with behavior change. She actually had a younger sister with children who lived an hour away, and she had not even considered asking her for help. Competent Celia had just taken on the financial challenges. Eventually she agreed to ask her sister if she might be able to take on some responsibility for their mother's care, and to her surprise, her sister was willing and able to help in ways that relieved much of Celia's burden. Her sister volunteered to take their mother to medical appointments because she could bring her children and because she did not work outside her home. This extra help allowed Celia some extra time to relax or take a walk or just watch TV. It felt a bit scary to let go, but to her surprise it also felt great.*

ONGOING THERAPY

When our worried and exhausted clients face challenging situations in the future, their tendency to take on too much responsibility may reemerge. Connecting clients with resources and helping them evaluate the benefits of using resources changes that life path.

Transfer Your Worry to Another Person

This is a technique in which clients identify people who can give them valuable, trusted information about the problems they are coping with. In addition to family and friends, these resources might include attorneys, accountants, social workers, respite care, religious groups that have volunteers for help, and local chapters of national organizations for various illnesses. Utilizing resources not only will promote flexible problem-solving but also will broaden your clients' perspective on the situation. People who are trained to understand situations, whether they are legal, financial, or health-related, will automatically, in the process of evaluating and sharing thoughts, clarify your clients' values and the basis of decisions they are making. Encourage the worried and exhausted client to take their offers of help and decide later if it was a relief.

> *Celia had made a good connection with the senior-care consultant and I urged her to rely on that person for perspective on her mother's chronic health concerns and aging. Once Celia, with the help of the senior-care consultant, had addressed her values and some of the real issues, she had to pay attention to her tendency to ruminate about problems, real or feared. We went on to utilize the types of worry management techniques described in Chapters 8 and 9.*

Build Circuitry for Joy

Get into nature. Spend time with friends. Slow down and "smell the roses," as the saying goes. Relief begins with self-care but increases when one allows oneself time to relish experiences and take a break from work. Typically it's best to ease clients into this by encouraging them to take small "doses" of pleasure. Being in nature is a powerful restorative, but you don't have to take a week at Yosemite to get the benefit of the outdoors. Ask about nearby options: "Is there a park with a pond nearby where you could watch the sparkle of sun on water for a while, resting before finishing a walk?" Find out if the client lives near walking or bicycling trails, or even just has a green and leafy backyard. Even densely populated urban areas tend to protect some areas to give citizens a place where it is green.

Look into other options, too—perhaps your client would prefer taking time to bake from scratch, or arrange flowers, or just sit still listening to a great piece of music. Take the time to explore various ideas—remember, clients are getting over rigid thinking!

FINISHING UP

The worried and exhausted client may well revert to worrying and inflexible problem-solving in conditions of high stress. The goal for therapy is to help clients recognize this tendency and put into place reminders of how tiring life will be if they go too long trying to manage worrying with working.

Develop a Team

One way to deal with "backsliding" into exhaustion is to develop a "team"—a handful of people who are available to give the client feedback about whether his or her choices reflect good self-care. It may be a friend who agrees to remind the client to say "no" to a demanding family member, or a pastor who can help the client consider the negative side of "selfless" behavior.

Although having actual people as team members is best, clients can also write themselves a memo to be read during future times of stress.

Occasional Therapy

Make sure your worried and exhausted clients know they do not have to be at the stage of exhaustion to ask for your help, even for just one session, to reflect on a problem. I want my clients to know they can always come in for a tune-up!

TREATMENT SUMMARY FOR THE WORRIED AND EXHAUSTED CLIENT

Assessment

- Physical health—pay attention to high blood pressure, eating and nutrition problems (including weight gain or loss), and sleep problems
- Readiness to change—denial of burnout can be corrected with education and discussion to see where in the burnout cycle the client sees him- or herself
- Mental energy—assess whether the client is functioning at work or in life and whether the client is resilient or needs coping skills; work to loosen up stuck, rigid thinking

Therapeutic Relationship

Collaboration is the goal here. Value the client's wisdom and avoid judgment. A motivational interviewing style is often helpful to this end.

Addressing the Symptoms

Lifestyle issues are a major concern with these clients, and addressing them is a good place for therapy to begin. However, because rigid thinking is a hallmark of this combination of anxiety and depression, clients may be resistant to lifestyle changes. Encourage clients to start small, and promote change by educating clients about burnout and challenging cognitive errors.

Specific Therapy Tools for Change
- Do What You Think Is Best on This List (join with client's own wisdom about the best place to start)
- Education on burnout
- "What Are My Values?" (to begin to break through denial about exhaustion)
- What Is the Dichotomy? (about prioritizing values)
- There Is Always a Choice; Worry Well and Only Once (challenge cognitive rigidity and feeling "stuck")
- "Am I, and Only I, Responsible for This?"
- Contain Worry in Time
- Change Behavior, Change Cognitions (behavior change breaks rigid cognitions)
- Ask for Help, Allow for Help

Ongoing Therapy
- Transfer Your Worry to Another Person
- Build Circuitry for Joy

Finishing Up
- Develop a Team
- Come in for tune-ups

CHAPTER 7

THE QUIET AVOIDER

QUIET AVOIDERS are likely to be born shy and sensitive in temperament. Although in symptom appearance these clients have a lot in common with low-energy clients, it is social anxiety that dominates in these cases, and this should be the treatment focus. The following checklist indicates the main characteristics of quiet avoiders.

| | | | | | | | | | | | | | | | | | | | | | | | | | | | | | | | | | | | | | | | | | | | | | | | | | | | | | | | | |

_____ *Social anxiety or separation anxiety.* These show up early in life and dominate the experiences of the client.

_____ *Low tolerance for sensations of anxiety.* This means the client is at high risk to avoid whatever causes anxious feelings.

_____ *Somber, passive temperament.* Nothing gives the client a "kick out of life" and this makes the client appear depressed.

_____ *Persistent depression, periodic anxiety.* The client's depression is unremitting but the anxiety may come and go.

_____ *Avoidance of opportunities to advance or fulfill potential.* The client's social anxiety may deter him or her from taking the risks involved in pursuing opportunities to advance or fulfill potential.

_____ *Social reluctance in unfamiliar situations.* The client may have appropriate or warm relationships with family or close friends but withdraw from social interaction in unfamiliar situations.

_____ *Dependence on loved ones.* The client may depend on a parent, partner, or close friend for help in leaving his or her physical or social comfort zone.

_____ *Introversion.* Even if he or she is socially competent, the client is likely to be introverted.

_____ *Need for "down time."* The client may need time to recharge after being in high-stimulation environments or engaged with people for long periods of time.

||||||||||||||||||||||||||||||||||||||||||||||||||||||||||||||||||||||||||

Unlike most anxiety sufferers, quiet avoiders are passive from a very young age and are not excitable or enthusiastic in personality. Their neurobiological setup seems to be for low reward from normal social experiences, so they are not highly motivated to participate with others. In fact, they are frequently sensitive to the world around them and may be worn out after spending time in high-stimulation environments like classrooms or open office spaces. They are also more likely to be introverted than any other type of anxiety-and-depression sufferer, needing time alone to recharge. Their sensitivity to the reactions of people around them increases their anxiety about social scrutiny and fear of humiliation or rejection. They may cope by developing a secure relationship with another person upon whom they increasingly depend to accompany them on forays outside of their comfort zone. The comfort zone is particular to the client, but typically it has to do the degree of social exposure. For example, one client may feel comfortable going to a movie but not a party; another may not even feel comfortable at the movies and prefer to watch DVDs at home. In some cases, however, the comfort zone has more to do with the physical distance from the client's home or the means of traveling there.

Quiet avoiders have coped with their anxiety over time by avoiding situations that seem too anxiety-provoking, especially ones that call attention to them. They have trouble tolerating the sensation of anxiety, and this is probably determined as much by their biological sensitivity to the sensations as it is to their unwillingness to withstand them. Avoidance has worked to decrease their anxiety; however, they miss out on experiences that broaden social skills or abilities at work or in other arenas. Quiet avoiders may be successful in their careers or other endeavors, but even when they are, they still haven't lived up to their true potential. They dislike being the center of attention and having too much responsibility. As one client said to me, "I am just fine as I am. I have enough with just my husband and me in our apartment, doing our work and coming home to recharge."

One feature that leads to depression in these clients is the social isolation that increases as the quiet avoider moves through life. Once out of the school system, these clients are less likely to develop friendships with others and have less need to maintain the friendships they do have. They are not filled with joy naturally, being more inclined by temperament and neurochemistry to be somber, so the life experiences that most would perceive as fun, such as travel or trying a new job, do not motivate these clients to explore. As they avoid, they miss opportunities to develop their talents and abilities and may fall into depression, feeling inadequate or worthless as time passes.

A CASE OF THE QUIET AVOIDER

Carina, 30, an interior designer at a large furniture store, did not appear socially anxious at first glance. She was pleasant and well spoken in our first meetings, seeking help with what she described as "relationship problems." But socializing, even with colleagues on the job, exhausted her. Although she was always pleasant to customers who came to her, as their relationship was circumscribed by her role, she took a long time to "warm up to" new colleagues. Carina stated that she felt most comfortable with one-on-one time with longstanding friends, and preferred meeting up with them at restaurants or bars so she could leave when she needed to. But most of her time was spent at work and at home, where she could relax with her dogs and her boyfriend. Her family of origin was only peripherally involved in her daily life; parental drug abuse had caused her to stop seeing them years ago.

Carina wanted therapy "to become more independent" because she did not know if her relationship was going to last. Although she knew she would be fine financially and could live in the house without her partner, she worried that she would not be able to manage socially without his support. He initiated most of their social activities and literally made sure she got there, encouraging her to go and driving them both to the engagement, which she did not like to do. He also helped when she had to travel "too far from the house," which to her meant any travel that involved driving over bridges or on highways, as well as all forms of public transportation. The couple of times Carina had flown on vacation she'd taken a benzodiazepine, which she said was "worth it" to keep her boyfriend happy.

ASSESSMENT

Assessment of quiet avoiders is somewhat challenging because it involves looking at things that are not present—such as whether they are not participating in family celebrations, not going out with friends on a regular basis, not going to a workplace or interviewing for jobs, and not dating due to lack of interest. You will need to assess the client's level of motivation, degree of pleasure in contact with others and joy in life's activities, and need for more achievement in work or personal spheres. Deficiencies in those arenas pose the biggest treatment obstacles.

Physical Health

With the quiet avoider, the therapist should check on health issues that can affect energy: thyroid levels, vitamin levels, anemia, and so on. These clients are not going to be high-energy even with everything in place, but any energy boost they can get from improvement in their overall health will help with their energy for therapy.

Carina's health was only a minor concern because she had regular medical care that seemed appropriate. She had a thyroid issue that had been diagnosed several years ago and she saw a physician regularly.

Readiness to Change

Assessing quiet avoiders' readiness to change can be done by look-ing at how they have identified their problem.

* Do they see the problem as anxiety they want to get rid of? They may not be fully ready to take on life changes if they view the problem as being only about unwanted anx-iety rather than about their way of living. They may want to continue their avoidance behaviors—after all, they feel pretty good when successfully avoiding what distresses them—rather than change them. In some cases they may identify their depressed feelings as the problem, especially if their patterns of avoidance help them escape anxiety easily.
* Do they want help in making other people happier with them? If it is family members of quiet avoiders who want them to change, you must assess the client's own level of interest. I often see this with parents who want their adult children to be more outgoing and capable of better jobs, and with partners who want their quiet avoider to travel or socialize more.
* Do they seek treatment to develop a skill or ability? This motivation is valuable in promoting effort to change some aspect of their life. In these cases clients are usually seek-ing help for a work-related or relationship-related change. Motivation for treatment will be higher when clients know that their own avoidance is the heart of the problem.
* Is their desire to improve their quality of life? These clients will have the highest level of readiness to change. They are seeking therapy on their own behalf (rather than to make someone else happy) and they often will already know their goals.

Once you have assessed the client's readiness to change, therapy should focus on preparation to take action. Typically the quiet avoider is missing various skills that must be developed, and these skills must be identified. The skills might be small areas of missing experience (like how to host a party) or broader areas of social inexperience that lead them to hold back from interactions of various kinds. Therapy at this stage may focus on preparing the client to do something as small as returning a defective item to a store or as major as a job interview for a promotion.

> *Carina's readiness was a mixed bag. She was motivated to expand her life even if it meant some emotional discomfort, but she had defined her problem as dependence on her relationship and did not see it as an anxiety issue. I knew she could stay in her comfort zone if he left—simply going to work and coming home to stay in all evening. Expanding her social world without his support would mean defining the problem as her anxiety, not as a relationship issue. If therapy could help Carina redefine the problem, she would become more motivated to strengthen her social skills and change her inner dialogue as preparation to take action steps to get out alone.*

Mental Energy

Quiet avoiders tend to be passive. They are comfortable being alone, and this begins the spiral toward isolation that feeds depressed mood. Being alone is easier for these clients—there are no social challenges to deal with. But being alone means no companionship, either. Quiet avoiders' mental energy is part of this cycle: They are not so depressed that they cannot think about the situation, but they don't have much energy to devote to pushing back against their negative self-talk. Talking yourself out of avoiding and into participating requires some strong, active thinking. These clients are accustomed to giving in to their fears; they have not used cognitive muscle to get through their particular challenge. Therapy must focus on finding the motivation to stir up some mental energy and practicing with small steps to build strength for expanding experiences.

> *This came up when Carina had to stick with positive self-talk to manage anxiety about social encounters. She was generally low-energy, needing lots of "down time" to recuperate from a day of talking with clients and coworkers, so building her social confidence required smaller encounters that did not seem too daunting. Because she felt comfortable meeting close friends on a one-on-one basis, we decided to start there. Carina had mentioned that one of her new coworkers seemed like someone she might like to know better, so she decided to invite that coworker to join her for a drink with one of her friends. Having her close friend there made her feel more at ease. She scheduled the get-together for a weekend rather than after work, knowing that she could better enjoy the outing if she wasn't depleted from a day of social interaction at work.*

Health, readiness to change, and mental energy were bigger challenges with CJ, another quiet avoider.

> *CJ, age 25, had all the hallmarks of a quiet avoider. He had gotten a job right out of college, but quit it soon thereafter because he found it too stressful. When his minimal financial savings ran out, he decided to move in with his sister and her family, who lived in a different state, and began working from home as an IT consultant.*

Without friends in his new city, CJ began working extra hours to fill his time and became utterly worn out. Because he worked out of the house, he literally never went out. He stated that time with his sister's family was pleasant, but he had few other contacts, even with what had been a good group of friends in college. He said he had never had much interest in sex and had never been physically active or athletic.

Because his work schedule was deadline oriented, CJ had long stretches where he could "hide" his lack of output, sleeping 10 to 12 hours a day and working only during the afternoons. He used anxiety about upcoming deadlines to make himself perform. "It's only when my anxiety about losing my job is stronger than my tiredness that I get moving to finish the work," he said.

When asked about what he hoped would be different in his life, he stated that he would like a little more energy but could not really imagine what it would be like to be different. It wasn't that he didn't like people—he just didn't need much from others when he had his sister and her family to keep him company. He had no idea what might be enough fun to motivate him to overcome his anxiety.

With this kind of client, a physical exam to look at the low energy, lack of sexual interest, and excessive sleeping is a must. These can be consequences of the neurobiology of social anxiety, but they also can be caused or worsened by low testosterone, low vitamin levels, or sleep apnea. A physician might recommend a mildly stimulating drug such as bupropion to address this type of passive, low-energy, depressed state. Therapy with this kind of low-energy quiet avoider must progress in smaller steps, with a lot of attention to the client's motivation.

THERAPEUTIC RELATIONSHIP

This relationship is about balance: helping clients see their potential without pushing them to fulfill it too fast. They need successes to develop confidence, and moving too quickly undermines confidence if they are struggling to succeed. The hardest balance here is working to improve social competence, which will always involve some disappointments, and at the same time encouraging confidence. As these clients perceive the therapist as having the qualities they lack (social skills and self-confidence), they may feel inadequate in comparison. Their tendency to see themselves as unequal in the therapy relationship can be balanced by attention to their successes in meeting goals.

An additional dilemma is that these clients often come to therapy wanting direction on how to change. To their detriment, quiet avoiders often have not been pushed by their families or significant others to move out of their comfort zones. If we expect too much too fast, they will be uncomfortable. At the same time, we must accept their desire for change and demonstrate confidence in them. As a fairly directive therapist, especially when teaching specific techniques at the beginning of anxiety therapy, I have to make a point of avoiding having too much influence on clients' decisions about what they want, because they need to find their own goals and motivations. The therapeutic relationship has to leave space for clients to develop their goals while simultaneously encouraging their own self-confidence.

Therapists must also be cautious about recommending techniques that the quiet avoider will find too demanding. When this happens, clients will "try" the technique and then feel inadequate when they fail to accomplish it. This failure only worsens their depression, which has been fueled for years by feelings of inadequacy surrounding others' disappointment in their isolation and dependence. Treatment must enhance clients' sense of competence and confidence, and the therapy relationship must be more squarely collaborative at the outset than it is with other anxious clients who want input and ideas.

> *Carina's efforts to be less dependent on her boyfriend were going to change things for her but would also change that relationship. Having not met her boyfriend, I didn't know whether he would welcome more independence on her part or not—it was possible that he relished being depended upon. Although Carina probably hoped I would make decisions about what she should try and what she should do with her relationship, I was not in a position to decide what was best for her. Putting the ball in her court would itself move her toward the independence she said she desired.*

ADDRESSING THE SYMPTOMS

In general, therapy will include finding activities that will help clients get physically active and involved with other people, even in superficial ways, as this will increase their confidence and also bring a little pleasure into their lives. Raising pleasure will help motivate them to do what they are fearful of. Lifestyle issues are quite varied with quiet avoiders. Whereas some of these clients are good about diet and fitness, others are ordering pizza more than cooking for themselves. Some quiet avoiders have skills and talents they regularly use and others are more isolated. Exactly where you start depends significantly on where and how this client is involved in life.

Lifestyle

Physical activity makes people with depression feel better immediately because they did something for themselves. For quiet avoiders, low on energy and self-confidence, everything that will boost either should be on the table as a treatment technique. Again, remember that small steps are more likely to be maintained and built on, and activities that fit naturally into the client's life will be easier to follow through on.

> *Wanting to spend time with her boyfriend, Carina had gradually begun going to the gym less and less. This lack of exercise was something she now sought to change. Her dogs were a natural go-to for her. They needed to be walked, boyfriend or no boyfriend. And this would serve two purposes: It would give her more exercise if she walked them one at a time and for longer periods, and it would get her out of the house and let her practice expanding her range of distance from home with her pets for company. Getting out to walk the dogs each day also gave Carina some natural down time after interacting with people all day. When she and her boyfriend eventually broke up, she had a good habit underway that helped her transition from work to home.*

CJ's isolation was harder to tackle, but we eventually hit on a solution.

> *CJ had become very stuck in a pattern of rarely going out. But during one session in which he described enjoying time with his niece, I stumbled onto the idea of taking her to the park for a while after school or dinner. This got him out of the house and interacting with someone else, and it boosted both his energy level and his sense of self-efficacy.*

Specific Therapy Tools for Change

Specific therapy tools focus on three main goals: changing inner dialogue, changing behavior, and changing cognitions. (A final therapy tool on dealing with driving or travel phobia is included at the end of this section, as many quiet avoiders have problems in this area.)

In terms of inner dialogue, we all have a script we play out in our head, even when we aren't fully conscious of it. Quiet avoiders, however, tend to be particularly unaware of their inner dialogues. Typically their dialogue includes self-statements that are catastrophic (such as "I will be rejected!") or that emphasize the inevitability of being observed and found wanting. It is useful to ask these clients to verbalize their self-statements, especially those about the outcome of trying something unfamiliar. The outcomes they identify are usually related to feeling anxious and needing to escape that sensation, or to appearing foolish in the eyes of others. The fear of humiliation (being observed, exposed, and found wanting) is usually the ultimate catastrophe. Two techniques—What Happened Just Before? and Write a New Script—will help clients begin to change their self-talk.

Changing behavior in small steps is always a key feature of treatment with quiet avoiders. These clients may have little excitement about activities or hobbies, and this makes for low motivation to do anything beyond what already feels safe. Yet often a little searching through clients' backgrounds will reveal activities that once held their interest, and therapy can focus on reestablishing those activities. The technique Rediscover Old Interests will help clients do just that.

Changing cognitions is necessary if one is to make any significant behavior change. There are several common cognitive errors that tend to crop up with quiet avoiders:

- "I am the only one who suffers this or has social fear."
- "I am the only one who makes mistakes (and mistakes make me a bad person)."
- "Everyone is watching and waiting to judge me."
- "If people are laughing, they are laughing at me." (misattribution of cause)
- "I will make a mistake and everyone will laugh at me or reject me." (overestimation of failure or humiliation)
- "I won't be able to handle the situation."

Two techniques—See Successes and Posit Positive Expectations—will help correct these cognitive errors.

What Happened Just Before?

Used in the same way as the Panic Diary (see Chapter 5), this technique helps clients identify the inner dialogue they were having just before they got anxious enough to want to escape the situation. Self-statements may revolve around fears of being observed, making mistakes, failing in a task, or simply feeling too anxious (e.g., "I can't stand this!"). Once clients have identified these kinds of self-statements, they can go on to the next technique, Write a New Script.

Write a New Script

Writing a new script involves awareness of competence for whatever the situation is ("I can handle it") as well as an acknowledgment that if a mistake is made, it can be corrected or survived ("and if I mess it up, I will live through it"). The script may also include: "I am competent to handle most situations entirely on my own, but if I cannot handle a situation, I can ask for help." Help clients practice the dialogue by imagining specific situations in which they are afraid to fail, and help them find examples of past competence in their lives. Writing the new dialogue on some version of "cue cards" and reading it daily will also be a good reminder of competence.

Rediscover Old Interests

This technique is about changing behavior in small steps. Search through the client's history to find activities that he or she spent leisure or social time on. When you locate something that holds the client's interest, identify a way to bring it into his or her daily life. For example, someone who played soccer in high school may not be able to join an adult team but might consider bicycling out of doors instead of on his Exercycle at home. A cook might be encouraged to find the local open-air market to shop; someone who likes to read might go to the library or a bookstore rather than shopping online for books. Maintaining and raising interest in an activity relies on actually doing it, so finding a small thing that the client can follow through on is critical. The spark of novelty will diminish depressed feelings and give clients new things to talk about with family or acquaintances.

> *Carina identified a few things she would probably enjoy, one of which was window-shopping. As a decorator, she would find any window display visually interesting, no matter what she was looking at. She decided that at least once a week she would stop somewhere to look at stores and see what they sold and how they displayed it. This would have the added benefit of keeping her from going straight home and would give her something of her own to think about and talk about with her boyfriend and her friends.*
>
> *It was harder to get CJ to consider small behavior changes. He was so isolated that there were few incentives to draw on. He*

told me he did not eat meals with his sister's family, despite their willingness to include him. Instead, he often ate alone or sat in the kitchen with the newspaper while he ate. He also declined to join them to watch TV. At first CJ simply agreed to start joining them for meals on weekends and to watch TV or play a video game with them a couple of times each week. These simple changes helped him feel less isolated and he began to talk with his sister about whether he should look for a different job. He felt relieved and less anxious when she encouraged him to do so but said he could live with them as long as he liked.

See Successes

This technique helps clients begin to break into cognitive errors, which often revolve around themes of failure or inability. Most people have days with successes, but these successes may get forgotten when people focus on glitches in their performance. Paying attention to what is working will increase clients' confidence in their competence. Days at work that go fine, time with family or friends that is comfortable—these are usually far more common than embarrassing situations and mistakes, and they need to be highlighted. Clients should be encouraged to change cognitions from, for example, "having difficulties means I am incompetent" to "everyone faces difficulties and I can successfully cope with them, too." That is a major goal with the quiet avoider, who often feels inadequate.

Posit Positive Expectations

Deliberately planning to counter negative expectations requires naming the ways in which clients fear they will fail (usually in a specific situation like a job interview) and then positing a positive expectation that they will apply every time they have a negative thought. It helps to write down these positive expectations in a place that is readily visible, whether it's on an electronic device or a piece of paper.

> *Carina's main cognitive errors were the beliefs that she wouldn't be interesting to other people in a social encounter and that she couldn't cope with everyday experiences like being too far from home. She also underestimated her ability to cope if things did go wrong. When we looked at experiences she'd had when things went wrong in the past, she was surprised at how many times she'd done well in getting through them. Especially at work, she showed flexibility and creativity in problem-solving with her clients. Carina gradually began to see her successes as real and more frequent than her failures, which increased her confidence.*

Driving and Travel Phobia

This phobia may manifest as an avoidance of driving, taking public transportation, flying, or traveling certain distances away from home, but once the phobia is in place, it needs to be addressed directly. The general way to handle driving or travel phobia in a situation is to make sure the client:

- Can stay calm
- Has the necessary competency (e.g., skill set to drive)
- Can effectively use positive self-talk

Once these factors are in place, the client can begin safe, short exposures that build confidence.

> *Carina was a competent driver who had begun to gradually restrict her range of driving because she feared not having control*

in unfamiliar situations. That led to her feel highly anxious and desperate to escape the sensation of anxiety. She was particularly fearful of getting trapped in traffic jams, especially on bridges or highways, where she couldn't turn off down a side street. She also disliked driving alone, as there was no one to take over if she suddenly felt anxious. As Carina's avoidance of driving became more severe, so too did her anxiety about the times she did drive. She needed to reverse that process by gradually increasing her range. I taught her to use a calming method of tapping on acupressure points to relieve anticipatory anxiety. She made sure her self-talk was a positive reality check: "I am an adult who is capable of handling a car and being alone in it." She then identified some routes to drive that felt safe enough to go farther from home. She was eventually able to get on the highway as long as it was not a toll road with long stretches of "no escape."

ONGOING THERAPY

Although quiet avoiders have different social needs, it is also true that they need some contact with others to feel fulfilled. Still, motivating these clients to expand their social contacts can be a challenge. With some clients the best place to start is with family relationships; with others it is established friendships. There are always ways that quiet avoiders can begin to relate to other people— whether it's through work, school, or community groups.

Adult-Education Classes

Adult-education classes can be a great way for quiet avoiders to begin engaging with others, even for clients who have completed their schooling. Community colleges and continuing education programs offer a plethora of classes on specific subjects from yoga to computers. Taking a class in a topic of some interest not only expands a skill set but also gives clients an opportunity to meet other people who share their interests. These classes are low-cost, risk-free ways to get out of one's shell. They aren't a guarantee of social contact but are one way to increase one's interest in the world and maybe meet someone new along the way.

Social Media

The impersonal nature of social media is not great for building relationships, but it's well tailored for socially anxious people who fear rejection. It is the primary way people share messages and information about their lives, and quiet avoiders can make excellent use of the various communication tools available. Making connections and extending invitations to get together is much easier over digital social-networking platforms, where rejections are less personal than those communicated voice to voice or face to face.

After she and her boyfriend split up, Carina reached out over Facebook to old friends, letting them know she was single again and developing some chatting skills in a way that posed little risk of failure. She was gratified to find that old friends still wanted to see her, and she got positive feedback about her work and her personal appearance. Not only did she reconnect with a girlfriend from her past, but she also connected with an old boyfriend— not an uncommon event when people start reaching out to old acquaintances.

CJ similarly used online communication to reach out to his former colleagues and, circuitously, to his boss. Without having to interview, he got an invitation to return to work in a new capacity at a satellite office that allowed him to continue living with his sister. Although he was extremely anxious about taking the job, he knew who his supervisor would be and accepted the offer. The new job would force him into the structured work life he needed if he was to make further positive changes.

FINISHING UP

It is not uncommon for new challenges to crop up just when clients think they are finished with their goals in therapy. As they feel better and enact behavior changes, others in their lives have reactions to those changes. The stronger your quiet avoider gets, the more likely it is that someone in his or her life will be unsettled by these changes and give some kind of "change back" message. Pay attention to that possibility as therapy progresses.

Drug and Alcohol or Other Addiction Issues

If your clients have used alcohol or other drugs to dampen anxiety, this may be a time when they look more seriously at the impact of the substance use on their life. Be prepared to discuss clients' substance use, and carefully consider encouraging 12-step self-help programs. Quiet avoiders may be put off by the social nature of these programs; on the other hand, the programs are a great place to feel socially supported while in recovery.

This can also be a time when another person's addictive behavior begins showing up as a problem. As quiet avoiders become more assertive and less dependent, they may also become less tolerant of others' difficult behaviors. It is prudent to listen for these kinds of changes in relationships, whether those relationships are with parents, siblings, or significant others.

It May Not Be Over When It Is Over

Some issues won't be a big deal—until they are a big deal. Things like parenting, job promotions, or other circumstances that push clients out of their comfort zone may loom on the horizon. However, there is no way to really tackle those issues until they become relevant to your clients. Ultimately, as therapists, we have to accept what our clients want in their own lives. What may seem to us like a fulfilling life might not be what the client wants or is ready for. It is not up to us to set the agenda for the life we think our clients should lead.

> *CJ was feeling okay about his new job and living with his sister. He did not feel the need to broaden his social interactions beyond what he already got during the workday at the office, and he still expressed no interest in pursuing an intimate relationship with someone. It was possible, of course, that he would eventually meet someone who interested him enough to change these beliefs, and in that case he might need more supportive therapy to manage that new and unfamiliar kind of relationship. But for now, my therapy with him was done, and I had to respect his decision to stop at the stage he had chosen.*

TREATMENT SUMMARY FOR THE PANICKY AND DEPRESSED CLIENT

Assessment

- Physical health—no common health problems underlie this condition, but check for issues that can affect energy (thyroid, vitamin levels, anemia, etc.)
- Readiness to change—feelings of inadequacy and minimal need for social interaction can lead to low motivation
- Mental energy—low energy and low pleasure in life affect preparation to change

Therapeutic Relationship

Focus on collaborative effort to balance clients' need for help with their own competence, and sidestep clients' tendencies to shift decision-making responsibilities onto the therapist by helping them make their own decisions.

Addressing the Symptoms

Getting some exercise and getting out into the world can help boost energy and self-efficacy.

Specific Therapy Tools for Change

- What Happened Just Before? (identify negative self-talk)
- Write a New Script
- Rediscover Old Interests
- See Successes (build confidence in competence)
- Posit Positive Expectations (replace negative cognitions with positive ones)
- Driving and travel phobia (stay calm, ensure necessary competency, use positive self-talk, and begin safe, short exposures)

Ongoing Therapy

Adult-education classes
Social media

Finishing Up

- Be on the lookout for relationship changes and "change back" messages
- Addiction issues (including codependency)
- It may not be over when it is over (clients may leave with work undone; whether and when to take on more is up to them)

CHAPTER 8

THE HIGH-ENERGY ANXIOUS & DEPRESSED CLIENT

THE HIGH-ENERGY anxious and depressed client presents with an interesting combination of symptoms and personality traits. Anxiety is the primary complaint and most obvious symptom, but this is primarily because the client's high activity level masks his or her depression. Left untreated, this depression can significantly interfere with recovery from the anxiety. The following checklist indicates the main characteristics of the high-energy anxious and depressed client.

||||||||||||||||||||||||||||||||||||||||||||||||||||||||||||||||||||||||||

_____ *Lifestyle marked by high levels of activity and productivity.* The client is driven and accomplishment-oriented.

_____ *High anxiety in response to interrupted activity level.* If the client's activity level is interrupted by illness, injury, or other life circumstance, his or her anxiety will skyrocket.

_____ *History of trauma.* The client may have suffered one or more past traumas.

_____ *Tension-related physical problems.* The anxiety may manifest as headache, muscle pain, TMJ, stomach or digestive problems, or insomnia.

_____ *Perfectionism.* The client's strong fear of mistakes drives much of the anxiety.

_____ *Rumination.* There is a strong ruminative quality to the client's anxiety.

_____ *Underlying negative emotional states.* These are suppressed or deflected by the client's constant busyness.

_____ *Underlying depression.* This is masked by the client's energy and shows up mostly in pessimism.

High-energy anxious and depressed clients typically have been high-energy since childhood. Probably "wired" with the neurobiology to be high-drive, they get rewarded for their accomplishments, which motivates them to increase their high activity even more. Over time, they find that they feel uncomfortable if they cannot be busy. They may develop an identity based in their high productivity, with a self-image of success based in taking action. Many of their relationships depend on their high activity. Of course, none of this high activity is problematic in and of itself.

However, naturally high on norepinephrine as they are, these people may move from being mentally alert and physically tight to being vigilant when stress boosts their norepinephrine level even further. They start scanning the world for signs of incoming trouble for which they should be taking action—action being their normal response to stress. This vigilance translates into a constant tension that is felt physically as a buzz of anxiety. Finding that activity relieves that state of anxiety—"I am doing something about it"—these clients fall victim to a vicious cycle of feeling anxious, being active to relieve it, having the anxiety return, and getting even more active. When high activity inevitably fails to relieve the anxiety, these clients start to believe they cannot stand life with this level of acute anxiety.

High-energy anxious and depressed clients have learned to cope with negative experiences and uncomfortable feelings (such as sadness, hurt, or frustration) by distracting themselves with increased busyness. At first such distraction can be a good thing: The client can get over a hurt or move into problem-solving. The risk in this way of coping is that clients may not pay enough attention to their emotional reactions, missing important information that could affect how they should respond (for example, failing to be appropriately on guard against people taking advantage of them, or being unaware that another person is draining their resources). When clients get to the point of feeling betrayed by others or drained of emotional or physical resources, it can increase their anxiety or trigger depression.

Clients may also get depressed when they cannot control the various life situations they believe are causing their anxiety. When their efforts to control fail, they start to feel inadequate and powerless. Depression is exacerbated when their high productivity cannot solve a significant problem, and a sense of helplessness sets in. Clients may be prompted to enter therapy when a specific situation disrupts their balancing act and their anxiety spins out of control. This frequently happens when an injury, illness, or other life circumstance prevents the client from maintaining a high activity level. Without their familiar means of coping, clients find their anxiety escalating to an almost unendurable level.

A CASE OF THE HIGH-ENERGY ANXIOUS AND DEPRESSED CLIENT

Carole, age 44, had no idea she was depressed when she came to see me for "jumping-out-of-my-skin anxiety" after she lost her job in a downsizing. She was single, with a 17-year-old son and a 14-year-old daughter, and had been divorced for several years. She had a "friend with benefits" relationship with a man she really liked, but she did not expect to marry because of the demands of work and children.

Although she had a severance package that would tide her over for some time, Carole had already lined up several interviews and said it was nerve-wracking to be without a replacement job. She said she spent most of the day fretting about needing a job and ruminating on all the "what if's" ("What if I don't get a job in time?" "What if I have to move for a new job?" "What if I can't get a good enough salary?" and so on). The extra time she had at home made her feel frustrated and powerless, even though she had many activities to occupy her: She was a volunteer administrator at a weekend food pantry, in charge of supervising the workers as well as soliciting donations and advertising the organization's services. She was also a "band booster" president at her son's high school, and did all the usual activities a single mother does with two teens living at home. She fully anticipated that she would lose her community and everything she'd worked to develop when she had to take a new job. "Getting laid off has completely turned my life upside down," she said. "And with the economy being what it is, I probably won't be able to find a new job that's comparable to the one I had."

ASSESSMENT

Don't be misled by this client's energy. The high activity level does a lot to mask these clients' emotional and mental anguish. Furthermore, clients may not be aware that they are using constant activity to distract themselves from this anguish. Assessment can be used to help clients see this process and begin what is often rapid progress through treatment.

Physical Health

There is no typical health-based cause of this client's anxiety and depression, nor a typical outcome of it. These clients tend to be careful about their health in general; if anything, they are overly attentive to it. Their anxiety combines with the pessimism of their depressed thinking, motivating them to get regular physicals or even dreaded exams like colonoscopies and mammograms. One thing is true for these clients: If they are faced with a real problem, they handle it well, so they search for real health problems and usually find them if they exist.

Readiness to Change

High-energy anxious and depressed clients are extremely motivated and prepared for treatment. They usually understand their part in their own troubles and genuinely want to be less anxious. Feelings of being unappreciated or exhausted are something they can talk about, but they need therapy to recognize that the demand for performance is self-imposed and not expected by the outside world. When these clients are in high-demand positions, they need to get more realistic about their abilities.

Despite this kind of self-awareness, however, these clients often do not see their underlying depression. Recognition of the depression may come only after treatment begins, when the client begins to discuss negative life experiences. And this recognition may spark a burst of new activity, sometimes even to the extent of interfering with therapy-session attendance.

> Carole was desperate to reduce her anxiety, but she saw no way to scale back her nonstop activity. "My kids rely on me to be a good parent," she said, "and I have to work to make a living." About her volunteer work at the food pantry, she said it "gave her more than she gave it." From her perspective, her busy life was something she couldn't change.

Mental Energy

Like high-anxiety clients, high-energy anxious and depressed clients have a good deal of mental energy. They often have the characteristic I dub "TMA"—too much activity—both mentally and physically. They try to handle their anxiety by anticipating and planning for potential problems, and they're good at that. But their energy is excessive, and when it becomes blocked, depression sets in, weighing the client down with discouraged and even helpless feelings.

However, this mental energy is a boon to any treatment plan you devise. Clients will quickly see where you are going and comply with persistence in trying the techniques you offer.

Trauma

It has been my experience that these clients commonly have a trauma in their history. It might be a natural disaster, a medical trauma, or some form of abuse. Although the trauma may not have been severe enough to suggest a diagnosis of posttraumatic stress disorder, it may undergird some of the client's high anxiety and tendency toward depression. Certainly not all high-energy anxious and depressed clients fit this description, but be on the lookout for feelings of helplessness or strong, disproportionate anxiety that wells up when clients' high energy fails them. These can be indicators that past feelings related to the trauma are being triggered.

Even when clients don't consider their prior experiences to be "traumatic enough" to contribute to their current anxiety and depression, traces of the effects of the trauma, such as helplessness, may undermine efforts to get past the anxiety or depression. In these clients, the impact of trauma feeds an underlying depression. Clients may appear to vacillate between anxiety and depression, with periods of high productivity punctuated by funks and discouragement about not accomplishing all they intend to. A clue to the trauma background is the surprising swiftness and intensity of the depressed mood.

Journaling, described later in the chapter, is one means of connecting current feelings of anxiety and depression to past experiences. Eye movement desensitization and reprocessing (EMDR) can also be helpful, especially for clients who downplay the lingering impact of past experiences, as the technique doesn't require clients to correctly identify how a trauma affected them. EMDR often illuminates the connection between an earlier trauma and the client's current surges of anxiety or depression. If you are not trained in EMDR, consider consulting someone who is and encouraging your client to do a session or two. Francine Shapiro's *Getting Past Your Past*, which is written for clients, is also a good resource.

THERAPEUTIC RELATIONSHIP

High-energy anxious and depressed clients are engaged and thus engaging—a good combination for establishing a strong working relationship. They will respect your ideas, value guidance, and be quick to work collaboratively with you. They are also open to guidance and not quick to feel judged or defensive.

However, because these clients truly value the achievements they accomplish with their energy, you must be careful not to suggest that you don't value all they do. They desperately need empathy for their situation, and they have no idea how to scale back their activity even if they know they probably should. They want your advice, but therein lies a pitfall: If you imply that there is something wrong with their high energy, you may lose them. A common response in this situation is to become defensive and dismissive of the therapist's suggestion to establish more balance in life.

To avoid this pitfall, empathically focus on how they feel and ask whether they are getting what they want from life. This will take them close to the pain that brought them into therapy without eliciting feelings that you are judging them. These clients are often judgmental of others who are not as productive, and they deeply fear being judged as wanting if they ever slow down or "take it easy." It is helpful to the relationship not to leap in with the idea of giving them permission to relax, as clients will often interpret this as a lack of understanding about the needs fulfilled by their activity. Convincing clients that you have their best interests at heart takes time.

ADDRESSING THE SYMPTOMS

These clients may look like they're headed for burnout, but they are generally "type-A hardy"—thriving on challenges and feeling a sense of reward in overcoming them. This ability to meet and overcome challenges is what keeps their depression at bay. They are reluctant to give up the very thing that has kept them from feeling depression or anxiety, so addressing the symptoms will involve balancing efforts to slow down and listen to themselves to identify disguised feelings with efforts to learn healthy ways to relieve anxiety and depression.

Lifestyle

The biggest factor here is balance. As clients strive to meet demands and be valued as productive people, their work becomes increasingly central until it is all there is. This is true whether your clients are CEOs, homemakers, students, or volunteers: They focus on work and squeeze relaxation, pleasure, and self-care out of their lives. The Balance Wheel—the first tool in the following section—helps clients reestablish balance in their daily life.

Specific Therapy Tools for Change

Achieving balance in life is a major goal of therapy with high-energy anxious and depressed clients, but changing cognitions and learning to identify and express emotions are important, too.

Changing cognitions focuses mainly on two goals: helping clients become more flexible problem-solvers, and addressing perfectionism. High-energy anxious and depressed clients are often prone to what I call "brain freeze"—when put on the spot for a fast answer or asked to switch gears abruptly, these clients freeze. They may say "no," resist irrationally, or dither about what to do. This stems from their high-norepinephrine, low-GABA neurochemical balance. These clients have amazing endurance but are not fast responders.

Another feature of the cognitive habits of high-energy anxious and depressed clients involves perfectionism. Starting at any age, even in childhood, these clients discover that their anxiety abates if they believe they have not made mistakes. What they don't understand is that their anxiety is not caused by making mistakes but rather by their neurochemistry—that's why the anxiety always creeps back. Not realizing this, these clients try harder and harder to be error-proof, and this begins a cycle of feeling anxious, avoiding mistakes, feeling relief, getting anxious, and trying harder to avoid mistakes. Eventually, depression looms, as mistakes make the client feel bad, wrong, or guilty. Therapy can address this problem by helping clients "talk back to" their perfectionism.

As mentioned earlier, high-energy anxious and depressed clients have learned to cope with negative experiences and uncomfortable feelings by distracting themselves with increased busyness. (This may be even more common with clients who have suffered a trauma.) Anger is often one of those uncomfortable feelings that clients try to ignore. It is sometimes said that depression is anger turned inward, and although that is not always true, for these clients it frequently seems to be the case. Anger can also fuel anxiety. Helping high-energy anxious and depressed clients identify and express their anger may be an important part of treatment.

The Balance Wheel

This tool is an assessment, an intervention, and a treatment-planning tool all in one. The full exercise is included in the Appendix, along with a chart to fill out, but here are the basics:

1. Keep track of every activity over a period of days.
2. Categorize those activities.
3. Rate the degree to which you are spending the desired effort or time on each category (some will be too much, others too little).
4. Plot the information on a wheel graph to see how balanced you are.
5. Identify specific behavioral corrections (e.g., add 30 minutes of walking 3 days a week) that will better balance your wheel.

The goal of this technique is twofold: to help clients identify what would constitute a balanced life, and to help clients examine whether they are fulfilling the goals of that life. When clients realize that they aren't spending enough time on a particular goal (e.g., nurturing family relationships) and spending too much time on another (e.g., work), they can redirect their behavior by eliminating certain activities and increasing others. When correctly balanced, these clients' high levels of activity will bring them less stress, more fulfillment, and more experiences of joy and pleasure, which may counteract negative, pessimistic thinking.

For Carole, the Balance Wheel was a real eye-opener. She had always prided herself on her ability to balance work, parenting, and community service, but what she hadn't realized was the degree to which she ignored her own needs. She rarely made room for things she valued: leisure time to read and socialize with her friends, and time to meditate and go to the gym. Although she still felt locked into commitments regarding her children and the food pantry, she could see that this opportunity of unemployment would give her some time to meditate and work out—she didn't have to spend every spare moment looking for another job. She hoped that as these new activities became a habit, she'd be better able to fit them in when she returned to full-time work.

"Give Me Just a Minute"

This tool helps clients deal with the "brain freeze" they experience when they are put on the spot or asked to switch gears abruptly. It entails (1) acknowledging and accepting that they might freeze, and (2) learning to say "give me just a minute."

> *Carole was on her way to an out-of-town track meet for her daughter when a worker at the food pantry called to say that two volunteers for that weekend had called in sick. Could she come in to cover them? Carole felt her anxiety immediately spike—she'd promised her daughter that she'd be at the meet, but obviously she was needed at the food pantry, too. Not knowing what to do, she used the "Give Me Just a Minute" tool, telling the worker, "Okay, let me think about this and I'll call you back." This gave her time to consider her options. She was still close enough to home that she could turn around and be at the food pantry before it opened, but if her daughter's track team didn't perform well during this meet, it might be their last of the season. She couldn't miss it. Then she remembered that a friend of hers had expressed an interest in getting involved with the food pantry—perhaps he would want to cover for the other volunteers. Just a couple of phone calls later, Carole had resolved the situation.*

Whether it's getting off the phone or waiting to respond to an email or text, taking time to pause and reflect helps clients become more flexible in their thinking. It's like disengaging the gears of a car in motion: "Give me a minute" puts the clutch in, disengages the spinning gears of their always-thinking mind, and allows them to shift gears and reengage.

Have a Plan B

If you have a Plan A, you must always have a Plan B—this is a necessity for clients who do not like to switch rapidly to another plan when something unexpected comes up. High-energy anxious and depressed clients may lose opportunities to have more enriched lives because their lack of spontaneity keeps them on their track, causing them to miss fun or exciting experiences that come their way. They might miss that terrific one-day-only performance at the art center because they planned to go grocery shopping instead, or not see the incredible underground cavern on the way to the national park because it was not on their agenda, or just miss a fun, spontaneous neighborhood gathering because they had to finish some chore at home. So, when they are planning anything—whether it's a dinner party, a work meeting, or a 3-week vacation—they should have a Plan B in place. This is an antidepressant tool as well as a way to manage the impact of high-energy anxiety. When a plan fails to go as expected, clients don't need to feel badly about it. Rather, they are ready to shift gears. There is less sense of failure and a greater sense of self-efficacy about everything they undertake.

"In My Life, What's the Difference Between Good Enough and Perfect?"

Encouraging clients to ask themselves this question helps them begin to adjust their attitude toward perfectionism. This is not a quick technique but rather a way of changing the way clients look at the world.

The crux of the technique is to figure out, in detail, what constitutes a "good enough" performance for the particular client. This may take some discussion, as different clients have different jobs, responsibilities, and expectations. (For example, someone cleaning an operating room will have to be more meticulous than someone cleaning a house for a dinner party.) It's quite unusual for these clients to report that they are satisfied with an "average" or "okay" evaluation of their work, and that's fine. The point is getting them to realize that there is a wide range between "average" and "perfect," and a performance that falls somewhere in that range may be "good enough."

Sometimes this involves a cost-benefit analysis. For example, suppose a person preparing a report for work gets about 90% of the report done in 30% of the time she devotes to it. When is it *really* necessary to spend 70% more time to get the report just 10% better? Is the cost of that extra time really worth the benefit of having the report perfect? In some cases, it may be—perhaps the client is being evaluated for a promotion based on the success of the report. More often, however, it's not.

> *Like many single parents, Carole constantly felt like she had to do more as a mother. This led to her overinvolvement with the band boosters for her son and to a hectic schedule of attending concerts, rehearsals, sports events, and other school activities. She also felt obligated to be generous in providing money, even when it stretched her budget. "I have to make up for their father, who rarely shows up," Carole said. "After all, I was the one who asked for the divorce. I can't let my kids down."*
>
> *Examining Carole's idea that she could make up for the deficiencies of another person gave her some relief. She had not realized the extent to which she felt she had to do the work of two parents, and she saw the fallacy of her belief that if she could be a perfect mother, her kids wouldn't notice their father's inadequacies.*

Is Perfection More Important Than Progress?

Procrastination can be a problem for high-energy anxious and depressed clients. Worried that they won't complete project perfectly or be able to do it all at one time, they decide to put it off until later. This helps relieve their anxiety, but it doesn't help the project get finished!

The key is to help clients understand that making progress toward their goal is more important than doing it perfectly. But even when they understand this, clients may still resist. Making slow progress toward a goal involves breaking the project into smaller tasks that can be spread out over time, and this contradicts the client's "do it all at once" plan. Remember, high-energy anxious and depressed clients may get "brain freeze" when they are challenged to do something in a way that differs from their original plan. They need time to slow down, switch gears, and think about alternative solutions.

But other issues may be at play, too. Does the client have the skill set needed to accomplish each task of the project? Does the client have a distorted sense of how long each task will take? Are there any problems with organization or planning? If so, these must be addressed.

Whatever the reason for the objection to the segmented approach, it is helpful to ask clients to answer their own objections. For example, perhaps your client is a student who insists that she can't write a paper over the course of several weeks because she'll "lose her train of thought." You might say in response, "Well, is there anything else you could do to keep yourself from losing your train of thought?" She might then come up with the idea to jot down her broader ideas about the paper in a separate notebook and refer back to the notebook when she sits down each day to write. Asking clients to answer their own objections connects them to their best skill—the ability to identify possible outcomes and plan solutions. It gets around the helplessness they feel when small obstacles trip them up, and it gives them more access to their competency. This also helps relieve their depression.

Cost-Benefit Analysis

The cost-benefit analysis can also be helpful in tackling procrastination. It makes spinning thoughts easier to sort out, and it provides a logical assessment of what clients are getting out of waiting and what their waiting costs them. With the student mentioned earlier, for example, one benefit of waiting and writing the paper all at one time is that the tone and rhythm of the writing will be more smooth and consistent. The cost of waiting is that she won't have as much time to do research and could therefore fail to include important material. Viewed in this light, the project would certainly suffer more from the procrastinating approach.

How Important Is the Task?

The high drive of high-energy anxious and depressed clients leads them to take on more than they can successfully handle. Because they are so competent, they're the first people others go to when something needs to get done. Disinclined to say "no" to requests for help, these clients end up with too much on their plate. Add their perfectionism to that equation, and you've got a bad combination. There's no way they can do a good enough job on everything, and their anxiety skyrockets.

The technique How Important Is This Task? asks clients to carefully evaluate whether the request is something they should agree to. There are three parts to the technique:

1. First, say, "Let me check and get back to you!" These clients' immediate inclination is to say "yes" to requests. Forcing themselves to wait to respond helps them take a moment to evaluate whether they really have the time and energy to take on another thing.

2. Next, ask, "How important is this task I'm being asked to do?" Clients will almost always say it's "very important"—but then, everything else they're doing is "very important" too!

3. Finally, make a list. "What will I have to give up if I take on this activity I'm being asked to do, and how important are those things I'll have to give up?" When they weigh these two things against each other—"how important is the activity I am about to take on" versus "how important are the things I will no longer be able to do"—clients will develop some perspective on the relative merits of the task they are about to add to their plate.

When another volunteer at the food pantry learned that Carole was unemployed, she asked her to "temporarily" take on an additional day of supervising. Carole felt cornered and compelled to say "yes," because "technically I have nothing else to do on that day." It was important for her to ask herself what she would not be doing if she agreed to the request. Once she clearly saw how much it would interrupt her job search, she was able to decline.

"If I Were Angry, What Would I Be Angry About?"

As mentioned earlier, high-energy anxious and depressed clients often hide feelings of anger behind their flurry of activity. When these clients do not express anger as you might expect, encourage them to ask themselves, "If I were angry, what might I be angry about?" the next time they feel intensely anxious. Have them quickly write a list of possibilities and bring the list back to therapy for a discussion.

The beauty of this question is that it is hypothetical—clients can disavow anything on their list when they have finished writing it. It is not a "to do" list of people they need to confront. Because the answers to the question are so wide-ranging, it is hard to predict how this method will affect the direction of treatment, but I typically find that it leads to productive discussion that ultimately lowers anxiety and depression.

> *Carole found her worry escalating when her job search slowed down. She was following as many leads as she could, but there was not a lot of hiring in her field at the moment she was looking. Her generally secure finances did not soothe her: She had no trouble imagining it all falling apart! Occasionally she would feel a surge of anxiety, and I asked her to use this tool.*
>
> *She didn't have to wait long for an opportunity to generate a list. Normally good at interviewing, she had an intense bout of anxiety during a recent interview, and wrote her list as soon as it was over. What she realized was that the interviewer had asked several questions about her former job, seeming to imply that the loss of that job had been Carole's fault rather than a result of downsizing. Writing the list made Carole realize that she had felt anger toward the interviewer—anger that she had experienced as sudden and intense anxiety.*
>
> *The bigger surprise came when Carole brought the list to her next therapy session. As we talked about her anger at the interviewer, Carole began to connect it to how she'd felt as a child growing up with subtle, constant criticism from her mother. Her mother*

had always delivered critiques while smiling, adopting the guise of being "kind and helpful" and never appearing angry, which was "unladylike." Carole hadn't been allowed to act angry at home, and she certainly couldn't accuse her mother of insulting her when her mother had been so sweet. As a child, she'd found this confusing. The interviewer had unwittingly tapped into all that with her innuendos about Carole's performance. She may have been trying to step carefully around a tricky topic without intending to be insulting, but the experience was similar enough to Carole's past experiences that it triggered her unresolved anger at her mother, which felt like anxiety. Once Carole was better able to identify her feelings of anger, we could begin to work on expressing those feelings appropriately.

Journaling

This method was described more completely in Chapter 4, but it basically entails writing about emotions that seem excessive to the situation and connecting them to earlier experiences. This technique allows clients to explore how past traumatic experience is still affecting their reactions in everyday life.

Carole had a medical trauma in her background. Injured in a car accident at a young age, she had spent time hospitalized, in traction and in pain, with a fairly long but eventually good recovery. Now, when she felt constrained in any way, she became intensely anxious. She needed to learn how to identify when that was happening. In her current situation, stuck at home without a job to go to, she felt trapped and helpless, and this made her begin to feel discouraged. She was growing increasingly pessimistic about finding a new job, and she was becoming irritable at home. It was only when

she identified the connection to her trauma that we could work on
desensitizing her.

ONGOING THERAPY

Always a challenge in directing therapy is paying attention to your clients' learning styles and personalities. (See Chapter 10 for more on this.) In the case of the high-energy anxious and depressed client, a confounding factor may be introversion. We often think of introverts as quiet or lower-energy, but this is not always the case. High-energy anxious and depressed clients may appear sociable but in fact be in deep need of alone time to process everything that comes at them in a day. These clients can become depressed when they don't get enough time alone to process information.

Another factor to consider is whether the client is a "field-dependent" or "field-independent" learner. Field-dependent learners prefer to learn in social settings and tend to look at things globally. They don't particularly care for independent work and do best when teaching is more structured. Field-independent learners dislike group work and prefer to structure their own learning. They are more analytical and tend to focus on details rather than on the bigger picture.

These different learning styles affect how clients make decisions. Field-independent clients make decisions based more on fact and analysis of outcomes, whereas field-dependent clients think more about the interpersonal effects of their choices. They want to make choices that will have no negative impact on others, regardless of whether the choice is in their own best interest. High-energy anxious and depressed clients may spend considerable energy trying to make good choices and still feel as if they've failed if someone is not happy with their decision. This becomes a source of discouragement and depression.

> *Carole was field-dependent, and this presented a problem when she was offered a job that was high paying but would require evening work. She was hesitant to take the job because it would mean being less available to her children and giving up her volunteer activities at the high school. A field-independent person would make a decision like this by objectively looking at what would be best, and would not be upset if the choice was not perfect for everyone else. But for Carole, it was difficult to accept that making decisions that were correct for her but displeased others didn't make her a bad person. In therapy we discussed various situations in which other people made decisions in their own interest and whether she thought those decisions were appropriate. We also discussed times when she tried to please everyone else and the outcome was not good for her (and often not as good for others as she expected). Then we analyzed this particular job decision. Carole began to see that taking the job was not going to hurt anyone and would be a good move for her. She probably would always want to please others, but she could begin taking her own needs into consideration, too.*

Additionally, field-dependent clients are highly sensitive to their external environment, whereas field-independent clients are more sensitive to their internal environment. As a result, field-dependent clients may find it harder to create time to recharge if there is disruption in their external environment. Thus, it is helpful for field-dependent clients to learn concrete strategies for creating alone time.

It may also be important to look at how clients process information. Asking a client who is more of a "thinker" than a "feeler" how he or she feels about things will not result in a helpful dialogue. Instead, try asking what he or she thinks about a situation, and then be quiet and give the client time to formulate a response. You may get a different, faster, and even helpfully analytic answer. Field-dependent clients who are social but introverted can begin to break their habit of focusing on how others may feel or react if you give them a structure to consider what is best for them.

Meditation and Active Relaxation

Meditation and active relaxation can be very useful for the high-energy anxious and depressed client who is not getting enough time away from people and situations to process. The challenge is that high-energy people often do not like sitting and meditating or doing relaxation, so you have to get creative about what might fit for them. Yoga is one excellent solution, as it provides meditative time in the format of using the body physically. (See Amy Weintraub's *Yoga for Depression* and *Yoga Skills for Therapists*.) Also consider physical workouts that have no social component—running, bicycling, and swimming, for example, are activities that relax the body and allow the mind to move creatively.

"What Can I Control Now, What Can I Control Later, and What Can I Never Control?"

These three questions, discussed in Chapter 4, may help mitigate the emotional distress clients feel when they are faced with making decisions that cannot please everyone. The idea that anything is in one's control could be worth some discussion, but these clients particularly need a reminder that they cannot control how others will feel about their actions. They can control their own behavior, they can control their impulses, and they can control whether they make considered choices. They cannot control how others behave or feel—a fact often lost on field-independent clients in particular, who may believe they have more influence over others than they actually do.

> *As therapy progressed, Carole began to see that she spent so much energy working to make others happy that she was rarely happy herself. She also had an inflated sense of responsibility for things that were out of her control, and whenever someone was displeased with a situation in which they were both involved, Carole felt as if she was to blame. For example, one night she had made a plan to go to a movie with a friend. She had picked the movie, and was upset to find that it had sold out when they arrived at the theater. They decided to see a different movie instead, but neither of them enjoyed it. Carole ruminated over how she was at fault for not thinking about the fact that the movie could be sold out, and she kept apologizing for it to her friend, who began to get annoyed by Carole's fretting over something so silly. To let go of the idea that she was at fault, we utilized the questions about control. Carole could logically see that she had no control over the movie selling out, and neither she nor her friend had considered that outcome. Also, it was not an important thing to fret about. It was still hard for Carole to see this as a neutral experience for which she was not to blame, but analyzing it helped, and eventually she was able to let it go.*

FINISHING UP

Although they are energetic, ready to change, and persistent in therapy, high-energy anxious and depressed clients still have a lot of habits to undo and new habits to form. This takes time. As the saying goes, "old habits die hard, and new habits grow slow."

Changing lifestyle habits, thinking habits, and information-processing habits will take time and require guidance though the rough spots.

These clients often benefit from extending therapy into biweekly and then monthly sessions over a long stretch of time. Changing lifestyle activities to achieve balance often takes months, and when life challenges come up, clients may revert to using their high energy to cover up negative emotions. Extended therapy also provides time for clients to identify and work through underlying issues, such as past trauma, that may catch them unawares and cause depressed feelings. Having a regular, planned therapy session helps clients stay accountable for their own wellbeing, but it also gives them access to a person who can support them through challenges, helping them avoid the pitfalls of helpless thinking or depressed pessimism that may prevent good problem-solving, until their new habits are solidly in place.

TREATMENT SUMMARY FOR THE HIGH-ENERGY ANXIOUS AND DEPRESSED CLIENT

Assessment

- Physical health—no typical underlying causes or outcomes of anxiety and depression; if anything, the client is over-zealous about health and regular checkups
- Readiness to change—the client is motivated and the beginning of therapy is usually uncomplicated; watch for the possibility that depression may trigger a burst of activity
- Mental energy—high mental energy helps the client complete treatment objectives

Trauma

Excessive responses when a client's high energy fails him or her may indicate a past trauma; consider EMDR treatment or journaling.

Therapeutic Relationship

These clients are willing collaborators and like advice, but avoid suggesting too early in treatment that they slow down. They will feel misunderstood. Express empathy for their dilemma until they realize on their own that they have to scale back activity.

Addressing the Symptoms

Lifestyle tends to be out of balance, with overwork no matter what the client's job.

Specific Therapy Tools for Change
- The Balance Wheel
- "Give Me Just a Minute" (when clients experience "brain freeze")
- Have a Plan B (to encourage cognitive flexibility)
- "In My Life, What's the Difference Between Good Enough and Perfect?" (to address perfectionism)
- "Is Perfection More Important Than Progress?" (addresses procrastination by encouraging clients to break projects into smaller segments and work over time)
- Cost-Benefit Analysis (identify the costs and benefits of procrastinating)
- How Important Is the Task? (helps clients say "no" to requests)
- "If I Were Angry, What Would I Be Angry About?"
- Journaling

Ongoing Therapy

Pay attention to clients' personalities and learning styles.

- Meditation and active relaxation
- "What Can I Control Now, What Can I Control Later, and What Can I Never Control?"

Finishing Up

Extend therapy to allow clients enough time to make lifestyle adjustments and to practice decision-making from a position of good self-care.

CHAPTER 9

THE HIGH-ANXIETY CLIENT

THE DISTRESS of persistent high anxiety is second only to that of a panic attack. And unlike panic, which comes and goes, high anxiety is unremitting, significantly impairing one's quality of life. The longer it persists, the more likely it is to create a state of depression. The following checklist indicates the main characteristics of the high-anxiety client.

||||||||||||||||||||||||||||||||||||||||||||||||||||||||||||||||||||||||||||

_____ *Dread felt in the gut.* The persistent state of anxiety is felt physically in the gut.

_____ *"Serial" worrying.* The client actively looks for external "causes" of the anxiety and attempts to eliminate them, only to find that the anxiety returns.

_____ *Worsening anxiety.* Good days without anxiety become less frequent over time.

_____ *Absence of pleasure and joy in life.* This is not because the client is incapable of feeling pleasure or joy, but rather because the high anxiety interferes with experiencing these feelings.

_____   *Depression resulting from anxiety.* The anxiety preexisted the depression; depression is an outcome of the anxiety.

_____   *High-level functioning.* The client typically continues to perform work functions well.

_____   *Tendency to be controlling and critical of others.* The client may try to allay anxiety by pushing his or her ideas about how to behave or do work onto every person in the client's sphere of influence.

_____   *Tendency to be excessively apologetic.* In addition to (or instead of) being controlling and critical, the client may be excessively apologetic as he or she frets over whether things are being done correctly.

_____   *Feelings of "absence."* Preoccupied by anxiety, the client may be unable to feel engaged in the present.

_____   *Increased anxiety during significant life transitions.* Significant life transitions such as having a baby, moving to a new town, getting a divorce, or getting a new job trigger higher levels of anxiety.

_____   *Irritability, impatience, and strained relationships.* Transitions raise anxiety, which causes irritability and impatience. This puts a strain on relationships.

||||||||||||||||||||||||||||||||||||||||||||||||||||||||||||||||||||||||

The high-anxiety client may be the most actively miserable client you ever meet. A combination of life circumstances and neurobiology create an intense, unremitting state of anxiety that is felt physically and emotionally. Clients with this kind of anxiety say things like, "If I knew I had to feel this way for the rest of my life, I would rather be dead." This doesn't reflect an intention to commit suicide but rather is an attempt to describe the intensity of their misery. It's not necessarily a statement of depression, either, but feeling this way for a long period of time will lead to depression on every level—physical, emotional, and mental.

High-anxiety clients are extremely preoccupied by their anxious worries. One younger client told me he had been "absent for every important occasion in my life." What he meant was that his state of anxiety prevented him from noticing life experiences like being vale-dictorian and winning awards throughout his university experience.

I often describe anxiety as the normal emotion people feel in response to ambiguity: When you don't know what's happening or don't know what to do about what's happening, you feel anxiety. High-anxiety clients feel anxiety even when there is no ambiguity, and their clever brains want to explain these powerful feelings. So they endlessly search for causes, asking "what if" questions until they land on a plausible (or semi-plausible) explanation for the state of arousal. But even when the "cause" they identify has some basis in reality, it's not in fact the true cause, and attempts to eliminate the cause do not relieve the anxiety. This only further intensifies the client's misery. With their body constantly telling them that "something is wrong," high-anxiety clients live in a persistent state of dread.

Because they spend so much time anxiously anticipating what could go wrong and planning solutions to potential problems, high-anxiety clients become excellent troubleshooters, project managers, and event planners. They can utilize their anxiety pro-ductively by looking for whatever could possibly go wrong and strat-egizing the best ways to prevent it or respond. That is the upside of their anxiety. However, that anticipation leads to pessimism, and as time goes on the pessimism becomes depression. With their anxiety causing the constant sensation that something is wrong, these clients eventually have trouble seeing any positives at all.

A CASE OF THE HIGH-ANXIETY CLIENT

Ryan, age 28, worked as a CPA. He and his wife had a 14-month daughter. He sought therapy because he could no longer stand the degree of anxiety he felt and was desperate for relief. His primary care physician had suggested medication, but Ryan was concerned about its side effects. Aside from his anxiety, he was in good health.

> *Ryan had never experienced a panic attack, but he felt the gut-wrenching sense that something was wrong almost daily. His stomach constantly ached, he felt weak, and his sleep was restless. "I work all night long in my dreams," he said. During most of his waking hours, his thoughts ran in circles about potential disasters. He described himself as being like a duck: "I look like I am gliding across life smoothly and calmly, but under the surface my legs are paddling like crazy!" He thought he would expire with exhaustion if this kept up. Having a child brought this feeling to an intensity that now was making him distractible and crabby—a bad combination for a new father who wanted to be a good dad and husband.*
>
> *Ryan said he had probably worried every day of his life. His parents had been inattentive and mired in their own problems: His mother drank and his father had trouble holding a job. They divorced when he was a young teen, but, in Ryan's words, "they hadn't really been there since I was 8 or so." He had good relationships with his five siblings (he was the youngest), but he rarely saw either parent. When*

asked what he worried about, he said, "It depends on the year." In college he worried about passing classes, after college he worried about getting a job, and after he got a job he worried about losing it. He worried about everything from being sick to not doing a good enough job installing a ceiling fan and electrocuting whoever turned it on. You name it, he could worry about it! He mostly worried about issues related to lack of competency, and every year offered more options for worry. Now they were mounting up and he couldn't shake them. Yet most people who knew him thought he "had it together."

ASSESSMENT

Although there may be underlying medical causes of their high anxiety, these clients are often too quick to attribute the anxiety to physical issues. The assessment should include an evaluation of health issues, but you should also look at whether the worry is serving a purpose or has been integrated into the client's perception of his or her identity, as these issues can impede quick response to treatment.

Physical Health

Medical conditions are among the many things high-anxiety clients worry about, and these worriers tend to overuse medical care because they feel physically bad so much of the time. Although they aren't hypochondriacal, they need reassurance that their symptoms are not signs of chronic or terminal illnesses. They also try to control anxiety with attention to their lifestyle habits.

As a result, high-anxiety clients tend to be in fairly good physical health. However, there are several things that should be checked for. One is adrenal function, which can create high physical agitation. Elevated thyroid can also make people feel jittery and anxious, as can vitamin B12 deficiency, which is not hard to check for. B12 is a culprit in high anxiety because it is necessary for nervous-system functioning. Things can interfere with its absorption at various ages of life, including anti-acid medications and insufficient intrinsic factor (especially in older adults). Because B12 is found exclusively in animal products, vegetarians may have less than they need. Other vitamins are also important to healthy function, but B12 is the more likely culprit for the high-anxiety client.

Other issues contributing to high anxiety include excess caffeine consumption and use of "energy drinks," stimulant medications such as drugs that treat asthma, or any product that promotes muscle growth (as might be used by bodybuilders). The therapist should also listen carefully for reports of alcohol or marijuana use. This may be the way clients manage to calm down at the end of a day.

> *Ryan's health did not seem to be causing his anxiety. He'd just had a physical to check vitamin B12 levels and thyroid and adrenal function, and he took no medications that might cause side effects of anxiety. He did not use much caffeine and did not use any drugs of abuse. He worried about becoming an addict, though, explaining that he drank a couple of beers every night to relax. "I never get drunk, but I do still worry," he said. "I don't want to end up like my mother."*

Readiness to Change

If any client is ready to spring into action in recovery, it is the high-anxiety client. They recognize the problem and know it is up to them to fix it—they just don't know exactly where to start. The primary stumbling block is a hesitance to give up worry that seems to serve some function. Worrying can serve many purposes, many of which client may not be aware of. This can interfere with readiness to change if clients don't recognize why they "need to worry." Clients may hang on to their worry for some of the following reasons:

- *A belief that worry prevents bad things from happening.* I call this "magical worrying." Clients logically know that worry is not preventive, but deep down they believe, "If I worry about it, it will never happen." I've even seen these clients resist getting medical checkups because they believe that if they go in, they will have the disease they fear. Trying to challenge this belief through rational argument doesn't work, because the belief is illogical—you cannot talk clients out of it. Instead, this might be the place to stress that anxiety is not logical or rational, so they cannot talk themselves out of it either. Worrying is an attempt to explain their anxious physical arousal ("I feel sick to my stomach; it must be because I'm about to get fired" or "I feel really jittery; it must be because my spouse is angry with me"). Whatever explanation the worrier comes up with, it often has little to do with reality. Consequently, the worry does not help and often makes anxiety worse.

- *An identity formation that normalizes the state of anxiety.* Clients may tell others (and themselves) "I am a worrier"—this seems to explain why they are so revved up and cannot refrain from mentioning their worries. When clients describe themselves like this, I often simply ask, "Do you want to keep that identity?" or "What would life be like if you were not a worrier?" Questions like these help clients begin to realize that they don't have to be worriers.

- *Relationships built around worry and reassurance.* Listen to clients' descriptions of important relationships with family and friends. They may have some relationships in which they worry and another person reassures them. These "reassurers" may feel that the relationship is threatened if they see the client becoming less anxious, and they may pressure the client not to change, usually without realizing they're doing it. At the same time, clients may not know how to emotionally connect in ways that don't revolve around reassurance, and therefore fear the loss of the relationship as the dynamic changes.

Ryan was tired of being drained by anxiety and feeling no pleasure or joy in a life that for all intents and purposes was a great one. Fortunately, his relationship with his wife was not one structured around his receiving reassurance from her—in fact, he tried to hide his worry as much as he could, both from her and from others. However, Ryan did admit that he sometimes felt that if he worried that something would happen, it probably would not end up happening. "It's like a superstition," he said. "If I worry that the fan I installed will electrocute someone, it might be less likely to actually happen. I know it doesn't make sense, because I would've installed it in the same way even if I weren't afraid of electrocuting someone," he conceded. "But I still worry about it."

To find out whether this was "magical worrying," I asked Ryan why he was worried about the fan despite knowing that he would install it in the same way were he to do it again. He thought a moment and then said, "Maybe it's because I feel like I'm not really capable of installing a fan. If I stop worrying about electrocuting someone, I might get lazy and make a mistake."

This comment was revealing. Although on the surface Ryan's worry seemed like "magical worrying," it actually was more rational: It helped him maintain the vigilance he felt he needed. Therapy would need to address the feeling of incompetence that motivated

this vigilance, as well as emphasize that it was this fear of incompe-
tency—not his supposed inability to install a fan—that was the root
of his anxiety.

Mental Energy

High-anxiety clients' energy is boon to treatment. Both actively
miserable and actively thinking, they can apply their energy toward
controlling anxiety. These clients are the most cooperative you will
ever treat: They will try every idea with persistence if they think it
might help.

THERAPEUTIC RELATIONSHIP

Of all the types of sufferers of comorbid anxiety and depression,
high-anxiety clients benefit most from an empathic, directive
therapy approach, and they accept suggestions and ideas with willingness. They are comfortable letting the therapist be an expert—
in fact, they prefer it at the outset because it allays their worry
about whether they have chosen a therapist well. This does not
mean you should not be collaborative with these clients, but you
should feel comfortable being quite directive at the beginning of
therapy. Setting goals can be done collaboratively, and you can ask
your clients about which methods they prefer to use. As the therapy progresses, the therapy relationship will become increasingly
collaborative.

One issue that is likely to emerge is that of self-trust. High-anxiety clients often doubt their own perceptions and may want the
therapist to validate them, and they may seek reassurance from the
therapist as well. This can be a problem when clients attempt to
transfer their need for a "relationship of reassurance" to the therapist
and don't focus on building their own confidence in themselves.

In the therapeutic relationship, take care to walk the line between being directive and assuming the role of reassurer. This involves reorienting clients toward trusting themselves and their own perceptions. Help them notice their ability to identify and resolve problems during the course of therapy. At the outset, the tool "If It's a Real Problem, I Won't Fail to Notice It" is very effective in helping clients begin to trust their own perceptions instead of seeking reassurance.

ADDRESSING THE SYMPTOMS

There are a lot of symptoms with this client, some of which can be treated with easy fixes that require little effort, like decreasing caffeine or sugar. Other treatment techniques, like thought-stopping, take time and "tweaking" in therapy. It is okay to do the easy things quickly and leap in with the most problematic symptom even right at the beginning.

Lifestyle

Relaxation is an important goal, but high-anxiety clients are never going to do it at the outset of therapy. They are too anxious to have fun, recharge, or rest. Relaxation should simply be established as a goal. At the beginning, it is necessary to ask about caffeine consumption, and you should continue to ask, as therapy progresses, about how they use alcohol to control anxiety (looking for present or incipient alcohol abuse).

Sleep Hygiene

Sleep disturbances are common among high-anxiety clients. They often have what I call "worry dreams"—clients don't go into R.E.M. cycles but rather sleep lightly and ruminate in their sleep about life's stressful moments. The moments are distorted in the dream and feel like insurmountable problems. The first two methods in the following section are helpful for dealing with this.

Specific Therapy Tools for Change

This section looks first at therapy tools for treating sleep disturbance and then focuses on techniques for changing cognitions (changing behavior is not usually of primary importance). The main goal is to interrupt and eliminate the rumination and serial worrying that are primary symptoms of high anxiety.

Ruminative worry—thinking the same worrisome thought over and over—reflects the underlying neurobiology of high norepinephrine and inefficient GABA transmission. Repetition of specific thoughts strengthens those thoughts, making falling into the "worry rut" more likely neurobiologically. Serial worrying is when one worry is easily replaced with another. The client feels a general state of anxiety and attempts to explain it by thinking of something to worry about ("I know I must have forgotten to pack something for the family vacation"). When that worry is resolved (the client checks the suitcases and finds nothing missing) another worry pops up to replace it ("I might have booked the airline tickets for the wrong date"). When that worry is resolved (the client checks the tickets) yet another pops up, and so on.

The basic method for interrupting rumination and serial worrying is Thought-Stopping and Thought-Replacing. This is a highly effective technique, but it is also challenging, as using the technique requires a considerable amount of willpower. I don't necessarily announce this to my clients, but eliminating rumination and serial worrying can take a significant period of time. Supporting clients in the effort is a goal of therapy. I tell clients that their worry did not emerge overnight, and getting rid of it will not happen overnight, either. They can feel somewhat better right away with Thought-Stopping and Thought-Replacing, but eliminating worrying completely might take some time.

As mentioned earlier, lack of self-trust is another cognitive issue that befalls many high-anxiety clients. This manifests mainly in two forms: a lack of confidence in their own perceptions, and a lack of confidence in their own competence. Three tools help with lack of confidence in their own perceptions: "If It's a Real Problem, I Won't Fail to Notice It," education on family systems, and Trust Your Own Perceptions.

Repeat a Counter Belief is used for lack of confidence in their own competence. Many high-anxiety clients come to view worry as a necessary precaution against mistakes. They fear that if they stop worrying, they will be careless, which could lead to all manner of trouble. This is especially a problem among people who were raised by minimally involved parents who did not spend time teaching their children basic life skills in areas like hygiene, cooking, cleaning, entertaining, or care of belongings. Repeat a Counter Belief helps correct the mistaken notion that worry is necessary.

Of course, there are situations for which the basic Thought-Stopping model doesn't really fit. When this is the case, there are several other cognitive tools to employ: Plan, Don't Worry; Pay Attention Out Loud; What's the Worst That Could Happen?; and What Is Possible Is Not Necessarily Probable.

Contain Your Worry

This imagery technique can be used in various situations, but it works particularly well for clients who have trouble falling asleep. It allows clients to get daily stresses off their mind so they can better relax into sleep. The basic process goes like this: The client sits with eyes closed, quietly breathing, and imagines an open container. As all the worries that are pressing on awareness or asking for attention come up, the client imagines putting them, one by one, into the open container. When no more things come up, the client imagines putting a lid on the container and putting it away somewhere outside the bedroom. Then the client tells him- or herself that nothing needs attention until the morning.

If the client doesn't like imagery, this method can be done concretely by writing down the worries and putting them in a real box or drawer outside the bedroom. As mentioned, this method works well in other situations, too, such as when the client needs to focus (for example, before taking a test or beginning a project) or make a transition (from home to school or work and vice versa). Children can use this technique, too, drawing or writing their worries as well as imagining them.

"What Can I Do in the Middle of the Night?"

People who have worry dreams say things like "I feel like I'm working in my sleep" or "I think about the same problem over and over and cannot solve it." These kinds of dreams will abate as the client diminishes generalized anxiety over time, but they are manageable in the moment with this specific method. When waking from a worry dream in the middle of the night, clients are to:

1. Get out of bed.
2. Shake off any grogginess.
3. Ask themselves, "Am I going to do anything about this in the middle of the night?" (The answer should be "no," unless the problem is something like checking to see if they left the oven on.)

4. Make a note about what they want to do about the problem in the morning.

5. Go back to sleep thinking about a pleasant topic.

Thought-Stopping and Thought-Replacing

This is the primary method for disrupting rumination and serial worrying. It involves saying "stop!" when worries arise, and then substituting the worry with other thoughts.

First, clients make a list of all their typical worries. Then they look at each worry, one by one, and evaluate whether there is any need to keep it. (Remember magical worry!) When they decide that there is no benefit to continuing the worry, they tell themselves that they're ready to be done with it and make a commitment to Thought-Stopping and Thought-Replacing.

Next, they plan on a daily basis what pleasant or productive thought they will use to replace the worried thought. When the worried thought comes up, they say "stop!" and immediately start thinking about the chosen thought replacement.

One of the worries that Ryan listed was "being a bad father." His concern mainly revolved around being too inattentive—he worried that he would fail to recognize one of the baby's needs and that she would suffer some horrible consequence. This worry had come to a head in advance of a weekend trip his wife planned to take to visit her ailing mother. It would be the first time she was away from the baby for more than a couple of hours.

After we discussed Ryan's ability to perform basic childcare tasks like changing diapers and feeding, he needed to believe his worries were unnecessary. He convinced himself of this by repeating the statements "I've taken care of my daughter just fine when my wife is at home, and I'll be able to do it on my own, too," and "If I really weren't able to take care of the baby, my wife would never feel comfortable leaving me alone with her" (both of which he believed). Whenever his anxiety spiked with worried thoughts about his caretaking, he said "stop!" and used replacement thoughts, which he had planned in advance, such as "What should I do with the evening once the baby is asleep?" and "Which movie would I rather watch this evening?" The weekend was still a stressful one for him, but none of the calamities he feared ever came to pass.

The real key to success with this method is persistence and consistency. Interrupting the worry only once in a while won't work—it must be consistently interrupted every time it comes up. And it won't go away in a day. But if clients are persistent in interrupting the worry over a period of time, they will eventually "erase the trace" of the worry.

"If It's a Real Problem, I Won't Fail to Notice It"

Again, this is a great tool to use at the outset of therapy, especially with clients who doubt their own perceptions and seek reassurance from the therapist. It's common for high-anxiety clients to believe that they can't tell the difference between worry and reality. But they can. This method helps them realize this. The process is simple: Discuss real problems the client has had in the past and how they differed from anxiety about potential problems. Then clients can remind themselves, "If it's a real problem, I won't fail to notice it, so I can give up worrying about potential problems. I can solve problems once they occur." Of course, anticipation of problems in the course of planning projects, events, vacations, and so on is still necessary, so I also teach clients that planning is not the same as worrying. (See the Plan, Don't Worry tool later in this chapter.)

Education About Family Systems

Many high-anxiety clients doubt themselves, but those who were raised in alcoholic families often have particular difficulty trusting their own perceptions. They may start to defer to what other people say, worrying that they themselves cannot tell what is correct. Their worries can become intense and cover a gamut of ambiguous situations, but parenting worries are often the most common. Because they had poor parental models themselves, these clients have a hard time knowing what is a reasonable parental concern. A high-anxiety parent might worry:

- "Can I tell if my child is *really* sick and needs a doctor?" Parents may sit up all night wondering whether to call the doctor if they think their child is unwell.
- "Are my kids safe? Have I prepared them well enough to recognize risks like poisonous plants or cleaning products?"
- "Do I know enough about food, hygiene, and so on to raise healthy children?"
- (in specific situations when children are away from home) "Did I ask enough questions about who is chaperoning or whether the amusement park has a good safety record? Is the summer camp really staffed with good people?"

Educating clients about how alcoholism or other problems affect family systems can be very helpful. When they know that there are typical issues faced by families, such as feeling responsible for the alcoholics' trouble with work or legal problems, they learn how to stop feeling so guilty when the addict is in trouble. Also, learning that children in alcoholic families also face predictable issues with overresponsibility and uncertainty can make it easier for clients to examine the impact of the family member's addiction on them. Claudia Black (2009) coined the expression that children of alcoholic families "don't talk, don't trust, don't feel," and this succinct description can open a discussion with adult children of alcoholics (and addicts) to see how they live this out. Not talking about their situations, not trusting their own perceptions (much less those of other people!), and not knowing how they feel is predictable. Normalizing it can make it easier for them to move forward.

> *Ryan had an especially hard time trusting himself. He and his siblings had essentially been left to fend for themselves, as their alcoholic mother was often sleeping instead of preparing meals or was gone from the house for days at a time. The process of eliminating Ryan's worrying required months of back-and-forth discussion about what he worried about, what he knew to be true, and how often he could trust his perceptions (which was always). We also did some insight-oriented work about his upbringing, and he attended Al-Anon meetings and read books about adult children of alcoholics to start learning about the impact of the alcoholic family system.*

Trust Your Own Perceptions

Because life has endless ambiguities, it is important for high-anxiety clients to begin to trust their own common sense and perceptions of situations. Following are a few ways to approach this:

- Review the client's past accurate perceptions (this helps clients achieve awareness that they are competent).
- When clients worry about whether they are doing things the right way, ask them whether they are able to read directions (such as those provided with new electronic equipment or in "how to" books like the "For Dummies" series).

Of course they are! (Obviously, if the client *does* have reading difficulties, a different intervention is needed.)

- Help clients learn how to conduct a time-limited Internet search on a topic, as well as identify reputable sources of information (e.g., understand the difference between the Mayo Clinic's online "symptom checker" and sites with user-provided content like www.ask.com).

Repeat a Counter Belief

This tool is for clients who doubt their own competence. The first step is identifying the belief underlying the lack of trust in self-competence—usually it's a version of "if I stop worrying, I will start making mistakes and mistakes are intolerable." Next, clients are asked to decide whether they need the belief. If they know they don't need the belief, the next step is to plan to repeat a counter belief whenever they notice they are worrying about making mistakes. This counter belief may be something like "I can be cautious and plan without worrying" or "everyone makes mistakes at times, and I can correct mistakes if I make them."

> *Ryan's worries were very persistent, and his efforts to do Thought-Stopping went slowly. Although he eventually became able to dismiss individual worries as insignificant, in general he was still afraid that if he stopped worrying, he would fail to notice something important and this would lead to a catastrophe. He worried about not worrying! His meta-cognition was "worrying is necessary," and it came in part from his childhood. The absence of parental guidance meant that he'd had to learn lots of life skills without formal instruction. So although he was competent in many areas—from cooking to home repair—he still questioned his abilities, because he'd learned them without training. When he feared he was not competent at some*

task, his counter-cognition was: "I can read and understand direc-
tions, I can tell when I do not understand what I read, and I know
how to ask questions to be sure I am competent." He also had another
counter-cognition: "Even though my parents did not show me how, I
have, on my own, adequately figured out how to handle most of life's
everyday problems."

Plan, Don't Worry

Consider this tool (and the ones that follow) when Thought-Stopping and Thought-Replacing don't seem to fit the situation. It can
be tremendous relief for high-anxiety clients to have clear guidance—in the form of a list of steps—on what to do next, whether
they're completing a project or planning a party or searching for a
new job. (If necessary, use a worksheet with instructions on how
to make a plan—many are readily available on the Internet.) For
clients who did not have parental guidance, this is a sort of parental
substitute, and it provides reassurance that they are doing things
the right way. It also provides a reality check for their perceptions
of whether they know what to do (which they doubt), because they
can see results as they complete each step. This tool also works as an
antidepressant, helping clients channel their pessimism about mistakes and failures into predicting difficulties and planning how to
handle them. As each step of the project is completed, they can see
that they have done well and reassure themselves about their ability
to correctly evaluate and plan for situations.

Pay Attention Out Loud

When there's no obvious cause for the worrier's feeling of high
anxiety, his or her brain will go into overdrive to think of something that might be wrong: "Did I forget to close those confiden-
tial computer files at work?" "Did I leave the oven on at home?"

On the way home from work, or on the way to work from home, the client must decide whether to alleviate the worry—but arrive late at his or her destination—by going back to check on the files or oven, or not be late but suffer anxiety about whatever needs to be checked.

A simple method of preventing this worry is Pay Attention Out Loud. Whenever clients are leaving a place (whether it's work, home, or school) they make sure to pay full attention to what they're doing, getting off the phone if they are talking, turning off the television or radio if it's on, and eliminating any other possible distraction. Then they talk out loud to themselves about whatever actions are needed to close up the office or house. Their ears will hear the words, and speaking aloud directs attention away from their preoccupied, worried thoughts and toward the tasks of closing up.

What's the Worst That Could Happen?

This is another method for focusing attention on a client's competencies. When clients define a problem, they generally can see that they know how to handle it—they are good at planning solutions, even for worst-case scenarios.

It may seem counterintuitive to ask a client plagued by fears of calamitous situations to identify the worst possible thing that could happen, but this question takes the client's thoughts out of the realm of worry and into the realm of planning, which calms fear.

> *Ryan's boss at work generally had a fairly hands-off managerial style, but on one occasion she asked Ryan to complete a task that he believed was meaningless and that would require an inordinate amount of time. Ryan didn't want to undertake the task, but he was afraid he would be fired if he did not adequately com-*

ply. When I asked him what the worst that could happen was, he realized that although getting fired would be a problem, it was far from a calamity. It might even bring him relief, especially because he and his wife had adequate savings to manage a period of unemployment.

This technique can also have the added benefit of helping clients realize that their worst fears may be a bit excessive. For example, I once treated a woman who suffered panic attacks when she found herself in a large crowd of people. When I asked her what the worst-case scenario would be, she said she was afraid she'd panic and pass out and that someone would call an ambulance. "And then what?" I asked. She paused. "The paramedics would take over and put me in the ambulance." "And then what?" I continued. "I would be in a hospital and my family would show up to see if I was okay." I asked again, "And then?" and she ruefully acknowledged that she would have to fess up that she'd had a panic attack and people overreacted. Her remarks helped dissipate her anxiety about her worst fear.

Once clients have identified the worst possible scenario, immediately proceed with the next method: What Is Possible Is Not Necessarily Probable.

What Is Possible Is Not Necessarily Probable

How likely is it that the client will really die from a panic attack? How likely is it that the client's 14-month-old will really starve to death because he hasn't fed her enough during his wife's weekend away from home? Of course, bad things do sometimes happen, and trying to convince high-anxiety clients that they won't is an exercise in futility. However, these clients are capable of making a reasonable, logical estimation of likely scenarios. Planning what to do if the worst happens, and then ascertaining how unlikely that event is to actually occur, provides profound worry relief.

That said, clients must think about this question deliberately, as they've often learned to doubt their own perceptions. A careful consideration of the likelihood of worst-case scenarios will help clients ground themselves in reality and learn to trust their perceptions.

ONGOING THERAPY

High-anxiety clients, doubtful about their perceptions and their competencies, may find a genuine lack of certain skills, such as parenting. They may have no model in their minds of how to parent or perform other aspects of regular daily life. They may even have a negative example.

Missing a Skill Does Not Mean You Can't Learn It

This is a crucial fact for high-anxiety clients to remember. Education can allay a great many worries. Through reading, community classes, consulting with friends or mentors, and so on, people can learn parenting, first aid, cooking, entertaining, job interviewing, basic sewing or home repair, gardening—you name it, there's a way to learn it!

> *I suggested some books about parenting and Ryan found a parenting class at the community health department to join. Talking with other parents helped him to see that his instincts were pretty good, and this was very reassuring for him.*

There Is No One Right Way—There Are Many Good Ways

Having to figure out life on their own has left these clients with a big misperception: that most other people know the "right" way to do things, and that they could learn the "right" way, too, if only the universe would give them that manual. These meta-cognitions must be continually challenged, and therapy must stress the fact that there are usually several ways to accomplish goals, all of which have pros and cons.

FINISHING UP

With high-anxiety clients, the end of therapy will approach only slowly, with clients reporting an increasing number of days when they feel good and are mostly worry-free. It's unlikely that clients will reach this stage in less than 6 months; 12 to 20 months (or even longer) is a more reasonable time frame. Therapy can end when the client feels that he or she is managing situations without falling into ruminative worry.

A Bad Day Is Just a Bad Day

It's not uncommon for high-anxiety clients to do well for an extended period of time but fall back into a state of intense worry when presented with a new challenge. It is not unusual for a prior worry to emerge. At this point their depressive pessimism will assert itself, with clients thinking, "I am back to square one" or "I will never get over this anxiety." This setback may take a few sessions to resolve; the focus should be on tempering clients' catastrophic thinking by emphasizing that a bad day is just a bad day (or that a bad week or month is just a bad week or month).

> *Ryan took a plunge into depression when he found out that his company would be downsizing with layoffs, and he spiraled into some of the worst anxiety he had ever felt. Despite having dispensed*

with this worry earlier, he relapsed into it once faced with what he perceived as the reality, rather than distant possibility, of losing his job. His worries went straight to the worst-case scenario of being unemployed, broke, evicted, and living out of his car. He needed some perspective on the problem, but he also needed to remember all of his tools to manage worry.

I Have the Necessary Tools

When anxiety pops back up, clients need to be reminded that they have the necessary tools to deal with the situation.

When Ryan's anxiety rebounded, we reemployed the methods What's the Worst That Could Happen? and What Is Possible Is Not Necessarily Probable. This helped him reconnect with his own competence to handle a problem. If he got to the point where he feared it was likely that he'd be laid off, he could Worry Well and Only Once (see Chapter 3). I did not reassure him that he would not lose his job, but rather reminded him that he could handle his anxiety no matter what transpired.

Booster Sessions

As therapy finishes, reassure clients that they have the tools they need, but remind them that as they feel better, they may forget to use them. Reassure them about their competence to handle their anxiety, and offer "booster" sessions if they start to worry. The longer clients go without needing to use these cognitive tools, the more likely a big stress will be to will knock them off their base. Coming in for a booster session or two should always be an option.

TREATMENT SUMMARY FOR THE HIGH-ANXIETY CLIENT

Assessment

- Physical health—culprits causing anxiety might include adrenal or thyroid problems, B12 deficiency, or medication side effects; get a complete physical and trust the results
- Readiness to change—the client is usually very ready and able to change, but watch for the underlying belief that he or she "needs to worry"
- Mental energy—mental energy is often high and an asset to psychotherapy

Therapeutic Relationship

Therapists must walk a fine line between being directive and assuming the role of reassurer.

Addressing the Symptoms

Restless or interrupted sleep is often an issue. Also check caffeine consumption and watch for alcohol use.

Specific Therapy Tools for Change

- Contain Your Worry
- "What Can I Do in the Middle of the Night?"
- Thought-Stopping and Thought-Replacing
- "If It's a Real Problem, I Won't Fail to Notice It"
- Education about family systems (learn origins of self-doubt and provide education about family system and alcoholism)
- Trust Your Own Perceptions
- Repeat a Counter Belief (to build trust in competence)
- Plan, Don't Worry

- Pay Attention Out Loud (when leaving work, home, or school)
- What's the Worst That Could Happen? (strengthens belief in competence and trust in perceptions)
- What Is Possible Is Not Necessarily Probable (scales back catastrophic thinking and grounds thoughts in reality)

Ongoing Therapy

- Missing a Skill Does Not Mean You Can't Learn It (skills training can be a valid part of therapy)
- There Is No One Right Way—There Are Many Good Ways (confront meta-cognitions about lack of competence and the rightness of other people)

Finishing Up

- A Bad Day Is Just a Bad Day (and doesn't mean the client is back to square one)
- I Have the Necessary Tools
- Booster sessions

CHAPTER 10

OVERARCHING THERAPY CONSIDERATIONS

In the preceding chapters I profiled the seven most common client types on the anxiety-depression spectrum, and the most effective tactics to treat them. But it's not always as simple as identifying a client type and administering the necessary treatment approach. Like in all therapy work, underlying factors such as temperament, learning style, personality type, accompanying addictions, and medication use inevitably come into play and affect how a patient responds to treatment. The factors I present in this chapter don't reflect pathology per se (with the exception of addictions), but they do influence the way clients take in information and utilize therapy homework. It's therefore important to understand how these factors may affect the client's progress and adjust treatment as necessary.

At the end of this chapter I will also present some alternative therapy treatments, such as guided imagery, that have been shown to alleviate symptoms of comorbid anxiety and depression. You may wish to incorporate them into your treatment program.

It bears repeating here that psychosis, severe mental health disturbances like bipolar I and schizophrenia, suicidality, posttraumatic stress disorder when it includes dissociation or flashbacks, and severe personality disorders are often accompanied by anxiety and depression, but the symptom-management strategies presented in this book do not pertain to these client populations. Originating in more serious and intractable problems of brain structure and function, these disorders will not improve from this sort of symptom-management therapy work, especially not without medication.

No one wants to be depressed or anxious, but for some people the recovery process goes more smoothly than for others. Clients who have an even temperament and no extreme personality characteristics experience their symptoms as unwelcome interferences in their lives and typically respond with consistent efforts to minimize or eradicate them. However, for clients whose temperament is more labile (i.e., emotional reactions vary easily) or whose personalities have a noticeable bent in a particular direction, therapy will have to accommodate those characteristics.

TEMPERAMENT

Thomas and Chess are notable researchers in the realm of temperament. They talk about temperament in terms of inborn characteristics that affect how we receive and perceive the world and how we express reactivity. Each person is born with a temperament that is fairly stable over time. Temperament traits can be seen in infancy and are evident in adulthood. No trait is good or bad, but some traits make it easier to be adaptable and flexible, which bodes well for getting along in a life and world that changes.

The aspects of temperament identified by Thomas and Chess include:

- *Activity.* Does this child display low or high physical energy and mental activity? Later in life, mental activity may relate to thinking processes, as well as to reading and reflecting.
- *Regularity or rhythmicity.* How predictable are a child's biological functions (waking, becoming tired, hunger, bowel movements)? People who are rhythmic may sleep better, be better able to predict their own needs, and be less irritable when changes occur in their physical schedule.
- *Initial reaction.* How does the child approach (or withdraw from) unfamiliar situations? (The child may appear shy, bold, cautious, etc.) The withdrawal tendency may make a person more prone to depression and will also affect withdrawal in the face of panic attacks or social anxiety.
- *Adaptability.* How long does it take the child to adjust to change? As they grow into adulthood, less adaptable people may find it hard to "go with the flow." They may be more stressed by inevitable changes of life circumstances. Social anxiety may be strongly affected by this trait. Adaptability also influences the degree to which clients embrace psychotherapy homework for anxiety.
- *Intensity.* What level of energy does the child demonstrate in both positive and negative responses? People who respond to the world intensely feel situations more keenly, which may increase the stress response both physically and emotionally. Their intense reactions may affect their inter-

personal relationships as well. Generalized anxiety can certainly be affected by this trait, as can negativity.

- *Mood.* All children display variety of mood, but are they generally inclined toward a happy or unhappy demeanor? It is not a surprise that happier children and adults tend to be less depressed and anxious.
- *Distractibility.* How readily is the child distracted by things? Although some distractibility can be a boon to creativity, it also can pose learning challenges.
- *Persistence and attention span.* How does the child handle frustration and how long will the child stay focused on a task? These qualities directly affect learning and achievement.
- *Sensitivity.* How easily is a child disturbed by changes in the environment? This sensory threshold might cause a child to be bothered by environmental stimuli like noises, textures, or light. This trait directly affects social anxiety.

How these characteristics affect a child's development depends on the ability of the parents to respond to the child's needs and help the child adapt in unfamiliar or challenging circumstances.

Some people are born with a temperament that makes them more vulnerable to anxiety and depression, especially if the style of the parents is not a good match. These clients might, for example, display irregularity, intensity of reaction, unhappy demeanor, and high sensitivity. Or they may show low activity, low adaptability, distractibility, easy frustration, and sensitivity. Such combinations may be very evident in low-energy clients and quiet avoiders.

Talking with anxious and depressed clients about having temperamental characteristics that make them more vulnerable may help them understand why the world seems so challenging. For example, people who are slow to warm up may see that they need time to adjust, which they can do quite well—just not instantaneously. As adults, they may be able to make adjustments in their environments or family activities that provide a better fit for their style and thus decrease the challenges of daily life.

Our clients' temperaments may not affect only the development of anxiety or depression but also their response to treatment. People who are easily overwhelmed by frustrations may find it hard to "stick it out" when they are trying to defeat worrying, and those who are by nature slow to warm up may need extra preparation to deal with situations that provoke social anxiety. A therapist who does not push these clients too quickly and who explains what is needed and then adjusts the pace of therapy to match the client's energy level and adaptability will find that clients progress more smoothly through treatment. In general, I find discussing temperament to be a nonjudgmental way of addressing clients' natural responses to the world around them. It is also helpful to discuss temperament when planning ways to make life less stressful.

PERSONALITY TYPE

Overall personality affects the development of anxiety and depression and also response to treatment. Personality is not the same as temperament. Whereas temperament is more about biology and neurobiology (which affect the reception of external stimuli and the person's response to them), personality is more about perception of self and interactions with others. The development of personality may be very shaped by temperamental traits.

Personality matters a lot in response to treatment because the issues that trigger depressive or anxious responses are often determined by clients' ability to adapt to changing situations, by their perceptions of their ability to manage those situations, by their capacity to enlist others as allies, and by their tendency to perceive others as the cause of their problems. When personality traits are strong, they interfere with creating modulated responses to new situations and with psychotherapeutic efforts to form different cognitive-behavioral patterns.

It is useful to consider aspects of personality that affect people across all types of anxiety and depression (those described in the Myers-Briggs Type Indicator). Although I don't want to give a treatise on that model of exploring personality type, I do want to identify a couple of points that are important in carrying out effective psychotherapy.

The types described by the Myers-Briggs Type Indicator (MBTI) are on four continua, three of which I comment on here, and these interact with one another to form clear and identifiable ways in which people take in, process, and react to the world. These types are inborn and preferred styles, as the temperament traits of Thomas and Chess are, but all people have the possibility of perceiving and acting from any of these points. Over the course of life people tend to process and act less definitively according to one type as they become more adaptive and flexible.

The MBTI aspects of type that affect therapy style are: extroversion/introversion, thinking/feeling, and judging/perceiving.

Extroversion/Introversion

In this model, extroverts are those who process information by turning outward: They talk to others and write about their issues to see what they think and to gain input from others. Contact with other people energizes them, and they thrive on active social lives.

They like work that involves interaction with others. Introverts process through turning to their inner resources and thinking things through before discussing what they think. Although they may be socially skilled, they find interacting with others, especially many at a time, exhausting. They prefer alone time to reflect and regroup.

These styles affect the therapy process. In some ways, extroverted clients find the therapy process more comfortable or understandable because they use the talking time to figure out how they feel and what they think. Therapists can easily see their process and these clients are interactive with the therapist. Their problems may be stubborn, and they may be as stuck in their anxiety and depression as introverts are, but talking about it helps, so talk therapy is a good fit.

The introverted client can use therapy every bit as well as an extroverted person, and in some ways may be better suited to a reflective style of doing therapy. A therapist may want to consider that introverts sometimes respond more slowly and thoughtfully to questions and may not put so much of their process into words. As an extrovert myself, I often have to remind myself to be quieter and wait longer for responses from these clients.

Depression and isolation often go hand in hand, circularly reinforcing each other. Clients who are introverted are likely to want more alone time and often will have structured their lives in ways that give them that needed alone time. Therapists should discuss with clients the degree to which alone time is comforting and restorative versus isolating. With anyone who is depressed, therapists should pay careful attention to the fact that isolated clients have no one who challenges their negative assumptions. Another big challenge, especially for single women, is that in isolation they feel lonely, and if they resort to drinking alone, no one will be there to notice or challenge their alcohol consumption.

As mentioned earlier, social introverts may appear to be very comfortable with others. When that's the case, listen carefully to how they feel about social engagements or how they feel at the end of a workday. If they work with people, their end-of-the-day exhaustion may seem disproportionate to their energy expenditure. Help them plan restorative alone time!

In anxiety-provoking situations, many clients seek reassurance. More extroverted clients, however, will have a greater need for reassurance from others. When they do not have enough contact with others, they may do more Internet searching or participate in online forums or chats. This can be quite destructive when it comes to defeating worry, as many people who are online are sharing fear rather than reassurance! Find reliable sources of reassurance for these clients who turn to others for support.

Thinking/Feeling

It is not true that thinkers do not have feelings, but their mode of working with information is more logical. When I realize I am working with a "thinker," I start asking what the client thinks instead of what he or she feels. I usually get the information I need to help the client move forward in treatment. An introverted thinker may need some time to come up with the answer, and this extroverted feeler of a therapist must exercise impulse control and wait for it!

Judging/Perceiving

This is the continuum that reflects how quickly people come to a conclusion, how much they want a plan, and how much they will stick to a plan. A person who is a strong "judger" may be more anxious than one who is a "perceiver" because life tends to shift and change and plans can't always be followed. Help these clients work with issues about control and be aware that they may feel any of life's changes as a threat to their equanimity, making them more anxious or irritable. Be sensitive to their need to have a therapy plan! They will better relax into the process if they have at least a general sense of your plan for their therapy.

Personality Disorders

The most recent edition of the Diagnostic and Statistical Manual of Mental Disorders (DSM-5) no longer categorizes personality disorders as somehow distinct from other mental health disorders, and has a rather more integrated view of personality, temperament, character, and cognitive characteristics. To be a diagnosable disorder, per the DSM, the client's traits must impair his or her functioning; personality disorder is identified by "impairments in personality (self and interpersonal) functioning and the presence of pathological personality traits" (American Psychiatric Association, 2013, p. 646).

- Paranoid, schizoid, and schizotypal personalities are severe disorders and are unlikely to be seen in treatment for anxiety and depression without evidence of severe symptom patterns.
- Antisocial personality disorders involve inflated grandiosity and a pervasive pattern of taking advantage of other people. These clients are not as likely to be in treatment for anxiety and depression.
- Borderline, histrionic, and narcissistic personalities may all show intense emotionality, impulsivity, internal feelings of

emptiness, and fear of rejection. Both anxiety and depression may occur in these less stable and more reactive clients. Of these three disorders, borderline personality disorder is the one most therapists see as being most likely to appear in therapy.

- Avoidant and dependent personalities are very focused on others and both have issues with external locus of control. These clients will be most vulnerable to anxiety.
- Obsessive-compulsive types are hyperfocused on details and are excessively stubborn, rigid, and moralistic. These clients are quite vulnerable to both anxiety and depression, as the world does not conform to their desired patterns of operation.

When clients show evidence of a personality disorder, prepare everyone involved for the possibility that therapy for anxiety and depression will not be fast. Clients with personality disorders can learn techniques about as quickly as anyone, but the challenges they face in coping with life's situations and interacting with others will make it difficult for them to see how to apply the methods. Therapy should revolve around learning new views of themselves and others, as their tenacious patterns of emotional or behavioral instability and inability to adapt will bring constant disruption to their progress. Normalize this in therapy. A lot of therapy time for anxiety and depression in personality disorders involves identifying what patterns are not working and what behaviors are in the range of the client's current style, and then broadening the client's outlook and skill range a little at a time. This may not solve the personality disorder, but diminishing the anxiety and depression may ameliorate some of the intrapersonal and interpersonal complaints.

LEARNING STYLE

Psychologist Herman Witkin studied cognitive styles: the ways in which people approach gathering information and solving problems. He worked on a conceptualization of cognitive styles called "field-dependent, field-independent" (see Chapter 8). Although this conceptualization is more related to learning and educational measure, it has some relevance to psychotherapy. Our clients' cognitive styles will influence their response to our presentation of information and their motivation for treatment.

Field and Social Interactions

There is a strong connection between cognitive style and social interactions. And a great deal of depression recovery and social anxiety recovery is focused on interactions with others. People who are field-dependent are frequently described as being adept at interpersonal relationships, having a well-developed ability to read social cues and to convey their own feelings. They may appear to be warm, friendly, and personable. However, people with this style may have weaker boundaries between themselves and their environment, and this can affect self-esteem and feelings of control. Low self-esteem and a poor sense of control over experiences can contribute to the development of depression and social anxiety and can stymie recovery. These clients may well feel the impact of their environment more than field-independent people do, and this can affect their level of stress. (These characteristics may also dovetail with extroversion and external locus of control, discussed in the next section.)

Consider the impact on treatment when clients who suffer from comorbid anxiety and depression exhibit a field-dependent cognitive style. They appear to be more dependent in personality and as a result, when addiction issues are present, these clients can easily become codependent. They are strongly predisposed to anxiety and depression because they find it more difficult to eliminate panic or social anxiety, to stand up to their worry, and to resist reassurance-seeking as an anxiety management strategy. These clients tend to feel depression as an outcome of their passivity. By looking at these field-dependent characteristics objectively, without assigning pathology, therapists can help clients see how these characteristics are influencing their behavior, and how challenges in their recovery are expected and understandable but manageable.

Those who are field-independent do not rely so much on external cues to understand information and make decisions. They easily impose their own sense of order in a situation that is lacking structure. Thus they may seem to be in control or controlling. They do not like to work in teams and may not be good candidates for group therapy, preferring to take responsibility for themselves and being relatively unconcerned about contributing to others unless it is necessary for problem resolution. They are not highly influenced by others when making decisions about how to take action, relying more on their own logic than on the thoughts, feelings, or opinions of those around them. They may seem task-oriented, similar to the high-anxiety client.

Field and Therapy

In general, when field-dependent people need information, they tend to look to other people, making them both responsive to and possibly reliant on therapy, a blessing and a curse to their recovery in life outside of counseling. They may rely heavily on ideas from the therapist (not a bad thing) but feel incapable of utilizing skills outside of the therapy office. They may also have trouble generalizing what they are learning to new situations in their environment. They may need to identify support people and structures for guidance when they are facing something new, and they often make excellent use of support groups and online therapy programs. Field-dependent people are sensitive to a lack of structure in the environment, making them likely to thrive in 12-step self-help programs.

Field-independent people look within themselves (like introverts and people with internal locus of control). This makes for a client who does not appear dependent but who may be self-blaming and frustrated with the anxiety or depression. Field-independent clients thrive on information that is fact-based and are more motivated when they are able to exert appropriate control.

Field and Stress

Field-dependent clients are highly sensitive to their external environment, whereas field-independent clients are more sensitive to their internal environment. As a result, field-dependent clients may find it harder to create time to recharge if there is disruption in their external environment. If they are introverts, they may need to be more sensitive to the need for stress-rebound time. Because they rely on information from others, therapy works best when it provides concrete strategies for creating alone time. Field-independent clients, whether extroverts or introverts, are more likely to take care of themselves when stressed. Their stresses often stem from situations in which their desired course of action is thwarted and they feel unable to control the situation. Learning about what is and is not in their control will help with stress management.

LOCUS OF CONTROL

Julian Rotter coined the term "locus of control" to refer to people's attitude about the amount of control they can exert over what happens to them. Clients with an internal locus of control believe they are responsible for the rewards they obtain—they believe their actions strongly influence outcomes. People with an external locus of control believe that their own choices do not particularly affect their life circumstances, and that situations are generally outside of their control.

In general, having an internal locus of control makes a person more resilient to stress and less likely to be depressed and anxious. However, those with a strong internal locus of control may be like our high-anxiety or high-energy clients, who tend to be very achievement-oriented and may suffer anxiety or get depressed by what they perceive as their failures. They may respond well to therapy, but they also often view their mental-health situation as a personal indictment rather than as a medical condition that they can influence but not control. With a very strong internal locus of control, these clients tend to want to control everything, which can exacerbate anxiety and depression in situations where control is not possible.

Those with an external locus of control tend to be more vulnerable to anxiety and depression because they do not believe they can control even their own thoughts or emotions. They may be slower to take therapeutic direction or encouragement to work with cognitive management or behavior change (this is true with social anxiety and panic in particular). There can be times when having an external locus of control is an advantage, however—particularly in situations where people need to be more easygoing. Not believing the world is in your control may help you accept situations and move on from them. It can also help people utilize mindfulness and meditation skills.

Try to present the idea of locus of control as a way of approaching control, and emphasize that both approaches have both positives and negatives. It is too easy to see the client with an external locus of control as dependent in an unproductive way.

OTHER CONDITIONS AND COMPLAINTS

There are several common disorders that may appear as anxiety, mask anxiety or depression, or develop as clients "self-medicate" in an attempt to relieve their uncomfortable feelings. Among these are personality disorder, bipolar disorder, and attention deficit disorder, but I want to specifically address high-functioning autism spectrum disorder (formerly known as Asperger's) and alcohol and marijuana use because these are common problems that may appear as anxiety but require different assessment or treatment.

Autism Spectrum Disorder

Many high-functioning people with an autism spectrum disorder (ASD) appear in treatment as anxious. In particular, they appear to have social anxiety (and possibly avoidant personality disorder). This disorder will be more noticeable after about age 8, when peer acceptance gains importance. In adults who have done well academically or financially, you might not be inclined to think about ASD, but people do not grow out of it. They adapt, sometimes quite well, but their anxiety results in "meltdowns" or outbursts and they are hard to soothe, being indifferent to logic or reassurance. Interpersonal relationships are likely to be strained.

High-functioning people with ASD may be bright and accomplished in circumscribed arenas, but their "people skills" are typically deficient. They may be shy or not, but even when they enjoy people, they may miss the social mark and appear self-centered or ungracious. The biggest issue in therapy is that they are often brought into treatment by family members and are puzzled by others' complaints about their lack of empathy, lack of understanding for others' needs, and so on. It is not that people with ASD don't care about others or their needs; rather, they do not grasp the social rules and reciprocity that others seem to understand without any instruction. Thus, even though they may agree to try different behavior, they seem unable to know when or why they should do what they agreed to. Any typical psychotherapy approach that relies on being able to talk about feelings and recognize the emotions of others will not be successful with this client.

You will observe many traits that seem like social anxiety with these clients, including:

- Social awkwardness, especially in unfamiliar situations
- High anxiety, both physical and cognitive, when asked to go outside their comfort zone
- Withdrawal from social situations when anxious
- Refusal to participate in normal situations such as parties, family gatherings, work functions, and meetings that are not absolutely required

ASD clients will not be responsive to treatment that would work for quiet avoiders or anyone else with social anxiety, primarily because people with social anxiety are able to learn social rules and adapt to them once they are able to participate in a situation with minimal anxiety. Therapists must take this into consideration when planning treatment with these clients. Table 10.1 charts observable differences between ASD and socially anxious clients and is relevant to both children and adults.

TABLE 10.1 **OBSERVABLE CHARACTERISTICS OF ASD
AND SOCIALLY ANXIOUS CLIENTS**

ASD	SOCIAL ANXIETY
underreactive to others' emotions	overreactive to others' emotions
cannot label emotions	can label emotions
social learning disability	socially inexperienced
cannot habituate to stimulation	can habituate to environmental stimulation
parallel play	interactive play
may be gregarious in childhood	always shy in childhood
BOTH	
have feelings and show feelings	
are sensitive to environmental stimulation	
prefer interacting with just one or two other people when there is a demand for interaction	

Addiction or Substance Abuse

If a client has an active addiction to a substance or behavior, that addiction gets first priority in any treatment plan. The issues of substance use and dependence are varied and are serious complications in any mental-health disorder and treatment plan. It is not possible to effectively recover while currently addicted. However, anxiety and depression can block a person from identifying and beginning treatment for addiction. When you know a person has a substance-abuse or addiction issue, it is appropriate to begin treatment for anxiety and depression with a goal of motivating the client and making it more possible for him or her to begin addiction recovery.

However, clients do not always reveal their use of a substance, and when you have limited or no collateral information, you need to listen for clues.

I want to specifically address alcohol and marijuana use. Although there are significant problems with other addictive drugs and behaviors, these two substances are so commonly used by people who are not addicted to them that their use in people with anxiety and depression can be misleading. Also, both marijuana and alcohol can have subsequent effects of increasing anxiety, which prompt the user to use more! This is how the addictive use cycle gets underway.

Alcohol

Both men and women cover anxiety with alcohol. Alcohol works in the brain very similarly to benzodiazepines (anti-anxiety agents). Among men, discussing their anxiety is regarded as socially inappropriate—they may receive scoffing or dismissive responses if they present these symptoms outside of the consultation room with a physician or psychotherapist. It is not unusual for men with alcohol addiction to have a preexisting anxiety disorder.

People with depression typically seek the blunting, euphoric effects of alcohol intoxication, but because tolerance develops to the effects of alcohol, over time they may become addicted to the substance. A particular challenge in treating depression when people are drinking is that alcohol worsens depression in several ways. Hangovers, sluggishness, decrements to health, and depressed mood are outcomes of excessive alcohol consumption. And if problems at work or in relationships develop because of it, those conditions worsen depression and limit social support for recovery.

Alcohol abuse among women with anxiety is particularly common. Women report more problems with anxiety and are diagnosed with anxiety disorders between two and four times as often as men. The issues I see most often are with women using alcohol to soothe anxiety, loneliness, and depression. It is easy to hide alcohol abuse or addiction under the guise of social drinking. And when women are single, there is less chance of a family member or friend providing feedback on their drinking or collateral information to a therapist. Women may drink alone after work or on days off, and it is easy for them to fool themselves about the quantities they are consuming.

I often see issues of misrepresentation of quantities and obfuscation of use in the outpatient population I serve. The easiest misrepresentation is quantity. When people tell me they drink "a couple of glasses of wine" I try to remember to ask what size glass. (A "one-drink" serving is 5 to 6 ounces.) When they say "a couple of beers" I ask them to tell me specifically how many. And then I ask whether they ever drink more than that. I've encountered one situation a few times in the recent past that would be funny were it not so serious: A woman tells me she has "two of the little bottles" of wine, which I assume are the size you get on an airplane or from a hotel-room refrigerator, until more careful questioning reveals that she means the 750ml size—which is small compared to the 1.5 liter bottle! Hmm. The importance of little details!

Marijuana

Marijuana use occurs across both genders and all ages of adolescents and adults with anxiety and depression. It is common but not often freely reported by people with anxiety and depression. Marijuana is not an anti-anxiety drug, but its effects include lightening of worry and depression, and it creates the carefree feeling that these clients find hard to achieve without drugs of abuse.

The argument about what constitutes addiction to marijuana is complicated, especially because there are some valid medical uses of it. Regardless, it is hard to talk about the negatives of marijuana with users because they just do not see them.

Whenever possible, obtaining collateral information about alcohol use, marijuana use, or other addictive behavior is desirable. When I do not have that information, especially with marijuana, I focus on clients' reasons for use and the possible negative outcomes of their use. The memory and health effects of marijuana do not generally concern users very much. People who use marijuana don't typically get into trouble like those who abuse alcohol and get DUIs, or into fights, or very sick from overconsumption. What will sometimes motivate a person to consider giving up marijuana (other than deteriorating school performance) is interference in interpersonal relationships. Marital or romantic partners may become irritated and ready to leave the marijuana user over issues such as lack of work ethic, disinterest in sex, changed involvement in family time, and so on. Those effects ultimately increase anxiety or depression, but one of the challenges of achieving abstinence includes anxiety without the use of the drug.

OTHER THERAPIES

The standard cognitive-behavioral psychotherapy approach I have discussed in this book may well be sufficient for treating many clients with anxiety and depression, even when therapy takes a longer period of time. But sometimes we have clients who just seem "stuck." They want to do better but don't make progress. Especially when we, as therapists, begin to feel that the hard work of therapy is being done by us and not by the client, it is time to step back and consider other treatment approaches.

I am wholeheartedly in favor of nontraditional therapies for depression and anxiety and urge my clients to pursue them when they are not responding quickly or effectively to psychotherapy. When I see clients who are not feeling any better after weeks of treatment, or who have not been able to do any of the homework or apply any of the techniques, I know they need something more. (I am talking here about clients without other complications such as trauma history or addiction issues, which necessitate different treatment plans.) When this is the case, other interventions can serve as excellent additions to the cognitive-behavioral psychotherapy approach.

But first, a quick note about medication, which is, of course, one of the most common adjuncts to psychotherapy. Like many other therapists, I often begin treatment with new clients who have already been put on medication by a primary-care physician. Drugs can, of course, be an important part of recovery, but I've been delighted to see a recent uptick in clients who want to try to tackle their symptoms without first resorting to medication. (Refer to the Appendix for thoughts on which medications are most useful in treating comorbid anxiety and depression.)

Other than medication, many physical interventions like herbs, supplements, hormones, and dietary changes can also help boost brain function in a number of ways. If you are trained and knowledgeable about these interventions, by all means work with clients directly on incorporating them. (See the Reading & Resources for further information.)

Motivational Interviewing

When clients are not utilizing action steps that I thought they were ready for, I use the motivational interviewing model to evaluate their motivation and progress. The first three stages of this model—

precontemplation, contemplation, and preparation for action—will help you get a sense of where your clients are.

Precontemplation

Do clients recognize that anxiety and depression are issues they have to deal with? For example, when a spouse initiates marital therapy and one of the major presenting complaints is the impact of the client's anxiety on the family, it is common for the anxious spouse to not see how the anxiety is a problem. Clients who are not taking charge of their own cognitions or actions may attribute their anxiety or depression to life circumstances and believe that if those circumstances changed, they would be able to stop worrying or feeling down in the dumps. Clients may say things like: "if only I had a good love relationship" or "if only everyone in this house would just start doing their part" or "if only I could get a job that pays better" or "if only my spouse would stop drinking." Therapy in this situation is focused on examining the connection between the various outcomes clients experience and their anxiety, depression, and behavior (and vice versa: how their life experiences affect their mood and thinking). For example, a mother may be so anxious that every small thing her child goes through, like a problem learning to read, becomes the sole focus of her thoughts. She therefore hounds him to work harder, making learning to read even more unpleasant for the child, and pesters the school for special services, making everyone around her upset.

Contemplation

In this stage clients are beginning to suspect that anxiety and depression play a role in their inability to have satisfying relationships or a good job situation, and they are beginning to realize that they might have different life experiences if they could only stop taking everything so seriously. But they still believe that if life would change, they would change. This is common among young women with depression who may suspect that if they were more cheerful and optimistic, people would like them better, but still believe that if they just could find someone to love them, they would immediately be cheerful forevermore.

Preparation for Action

In this stage, clients have accepted the fact that anxiety and depression are interfering in their lives and are ready to take the initial steps toward addressing them. Preparation for action varies from client to client, but it is a crucial and often challenging stage for clients with a trauma history or social anxiety. In the case of trauma history, therapy will focus on identifying and desensitizing triggers for panic or depressive plunges of mood. Clients may suffer setbacks at this stage while working on trauma recovery. (Eye movement desensitization and reprocessing and energy tapping, discussed in the following sections, as well as other desensitization techniques, can help make forward progress more consistent.) In the case of social anxiety, therapy will focus on providing whatever social skill set is needed. This may include teaching interviewing skills, performance-anxiety management, dating skills, or other skills necessary to competently navigate interpersonal worlds.

Eye Movement Desensitization and Reprocessing

Developed by Francine Shapiro, eye movement desensitization and reprocessing (EMDR) not only is an evidence-based psychotherapy for posttraumatic stress disorder but also is extremely useful for managing anticipatory anxiety, for discovering and desensitizing triggers for panic, social anxiety, and depressive "plunges," and for installing resources for competent social functioning. It is a valuable tool for all anxiety disorders and depression.

I utilize EMDR with almost every client who has a history of trauma. I would not advise therapists not trained in the method to use it with clients who have had serious traumatic experiences, however. That said, Dr. Shapiro's book *Getting Past Your Past* was written to bring the benefits of the EMDR method to the general public, and it may be great resource for those without training in EMDR.

Energy Tapping

This method goes by many names, including emotional self-management (ESM), thought-field therapy (TFT), and emotional freedom technique (EFT). It utilizes the understanding of energy from the Chinese approach to medicine, which examines the flow of energy through meridians of the body. Through that lens, emotional disturbance is seen as energy-flow disturbance that causes negative emotional reactions. When balance is restored, the negative arousal ceases. To balance energy, clients "tune in" to specific issues while tapping on meridian points with their fingertips.

This method is especially helpful for all types of anticipatory anxiety and for some kinds of negative memories. I also use it for clients who get stuck on worried thoughts and find it hard to use cognitive methods to dismiss them. Every client of mine learns to use tapping at some point during our treatment, and I encourage clients to utilize this method on their own and keep it as a relapse-prevention tool for life.

Hypnosis and Guided Imagery

Although I do not practice hypnosis or utilize guided imagery, I do refer clients to other professionals who specialize in these methods, knowing they have great value in treating many aspects of anxiety and depression. These tools have many applications, but I am most likely to refer clients to my colleagues when they have a "failure of will"—by their own definition. For example, a client may say she wants to exercise more (or start taking supplements, or quit smoking, or stop binging on sweets, etc.) but just can't figure out how to make herself do it.

Hypnosis

Hypnosis uses an altered state of awareness, called a "trance," to focus attention and concentration on a specific thought while blocking out other environmental stimuli. A skilled hypnotherapist can use the trance state to help people explore material that might be outside of their conscious awareness or to perceive things differently. It can also be used to create suggestions or to analyze situations. In this way it is an excellent aid to psychotherapy.

The hypnotic trance state makes a person more able to take in suggestions related to changing behavior (like quitting smoking), ignoring unnecessary signals of pain, or adding behaviors (such as work completion). When hypnosis is used for analysis, the hypnotherapist explores root causes of symptoms and may uncover aspects of the problem in a past trauma. Then psychotherapy can continue the work of desensitizing the trauma.

Guided Imagery

Belleruth Naparstek, one of the pioneers of guided imagery, described this method as "a gentle but powerful technique that focuses and directs the imagination" (Naparstek, 2000). The imagery can take many forms, depending on the client's needs: "It can be just as simple as an athlete's 10-second reverie, just before leaping off the diving board, imagining how a perfect dive feels when slicing through the water. Or it can be as complex as imagining the busy, focused buzz of thousands of loyal immune cells, scooting out of the thymus gland on a search and destroy mission to wipe out unsuspecting cancer cells" (Naparstek, 2000).

Often confused with "visualization" techniques, which are less complex and concentrate mainly on the visual sense, guided imagery engages the body-mind connection to address everything from health issues to performance in athletic or musical activities. Many clients have found it a helpful tool for reducing depression and anxiety and improving stress resilience.

Repetitive Transcranial Magnetic Stimulation

Repetitive transcranial magnetic stimulation (rTMS) was approved by the FDA in 2008 for depression, and research is beginning to show its efficacy for anxiety. I have referred clients for rTMS when I see that their anxiety and depression are reciprocally reinforcing and when rumination is painfully life-disturbing. The method is a noninvasive, nonconvulsive neurostimulation treatment that must be performed by a trained medical professional. Side effects of this treatment are typically minimal and easily tolerated.

My clients who have undergone rTMS have been surprised by the immediate changes in their ability to manage and dismiss anxious rumination and depressive states.

Neurofeedback

One idea about why depression and anxiety are so challenging to modulate is that brain function is disturbed at the level of electrical signaling. Like rTMS, neurofeedback addresses that. This noninvasive method uses moment-to-moment direct feedback from an EEG (a measure of electrical activity in the brain) to train the brain to self-regulate. Watching or listening to video or audio input (or both), the brain is rewarded for changing its own activity to more appropriate patterns. This is a gradual learning process.

Clients who are stuck may feel as if they cannot control their mood or their thoughts. Especially when they have low mental energy or excessive mental agitation, I encourage clients to investigate whether neurofeedback might be helpful. They can get an evaluation from a trained practitioner, who will show them the balance of activity in their brain and explain how neurofeedback might bring them into better balance.

CONSIDERATIONS FOR CONTINUING OR TERMINATING THERAPY

Life happens. Clients with anxiety and depression enter therapy when their ability to tolerate their symptoms or cope with life is impaired by their emotional state. Once they are on their way with symptom management, their progress through therapy depends on their individual ability to implement strategies. Some life issues that can interfere with progress, such as the impact of burnout, were addressed in previous chapters.

Regardless of client type, extenuating circumstances may make ongoing psychotherapy support advisable. Extended therapy can help clients maintain gains and prevent relapse in situations including:

- Divorce
- Illness or death of a family member
- Illness of the client
- Legal or school problems

- Job loss
- Addiction in a family member

The possible situations are myriad, and these kinds of stresses can easily provoke relapse. Relapse rates are in general quite high with anxiety and depression, but ongoing therapy can help clients cope with life challenges and develop resilience to future stresses. Honing the methods while dealing with life challenges is like getting on-the-job training.

Signs will appear when anxious and depressed clients are getting ready to finish therapy. If you have used a Beck or Hamilton anxiety or depression questionnaire to measure symptom severity, or if you have your own symptom checklist for signs of improvement, retesting will reveal less distress from symptoms. I prefer to assess where my clients are by using the motivational-interviewing concepts of action steps being completed and relapse prevention.

I typically see clients once a week for a 55-minute session. Relying on the clients' perceptions of how they are feeling and handling stress, I listen for evidence that they are mastering the tools to improve their emotional and behavioral state. When I hear each week that they managed well in a situation that they once would have found difficult, I know they are getting what they need, and unless life throws them a curveball, they are about ready to terminate therapy.

When clients can go through most of their daily life activities without feeling so depressed or anxious, we often decrease the frequency of therapy to every other week for a couple of months. During that time, we review skills and how they used them, talk about relapse prevention, and make sure they solidify lifestyle changes. Then we schedule a final therapy session for a month later to review their progress and their goals and to discuss under what circumstances they should come in for a booster session.

It's common for people facing a new stressor to return to their old means of coping, which might be withdrawal, isolation, worry, increased work activity, and so on. I don't want to alarm clients by predicting failure, but we do discuss that all people tend to falter under stress. I normalize a return to therapy by comparing it to a booster shot: Even things like tetanus shots lose their efficacy as time passes without the need for the antibodies. Like a new vaccination, booster sessions should be scheduled immediately when clients are struggling with a new life challenge. Whether it takes just one session or a few, a review of therapy tools and support in reapplying them will help clients maintain a life free from anxiety and depression.

THE BALANCE WHEEL

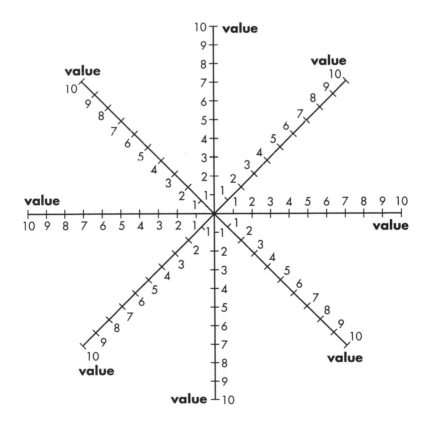

THE BALANCE Wheel is an exercise that assists clients in getting themselves back on track. As balance in one arena improves, balance in others will follow naturally, or at least be easier to achieve. The exercise takes a bit of time, but it is a great way to help clients express their values, identify what they believe would be an ideal balance, set goals, and examine if they are fulfilling their goals of a balanced life. Knowing where to begin a behavior change—and what actions are needed—is enormously helpful to restoring balance. The process involves 11 steps:

1. Make three columns on a sheet of paper.
2. In the first column, list every activity you do in one week. (You can do this over the course of the week, writing things down as you do them, or you can go back over the past week in your mind and write down everything you remember now.) Include everything, including sleep time and activities like washing dishes or taking a shower. You'll be the only one who reads the list, so don't leave out things like making love or anything else you may think "shouldn't" go on the list. You will see why this is important shortly.
3. In the second column, next to each item, write down why you did it. Let's say you stayed an hour later at work because your supervisor asked you to finish something today when you could have worked on it tomorrow. Why did you stay to do it? It might have been to earn the overtime, it might have been to please the supervisor or avoid conflict, or it might have been to demonstrate your effort to get a promotion. There may be many reasons—try to pick the most important.
4. In the third column, write the value that you associate with the reason you did it. Figuring out the value may be

the tricky part. In the example of staying for work, the overtime might be related to valuing financial stability. Avoiding conflict with the boss might be related to valuing peacefulness but might also be about keeping your job, which is ultimately about financial stability. Perhaps you stayed because you agreed that the work needed to be done and you value doing a good job at whatever you do. Here are some other examples: "I walked to work," "I took vitamins," and "I ate my vegetables every day." These different activities may reflect the same value: to take care of your health. Find a value associated with each different activity on your list.

5. Now consider what your *ideal fulfillment* of each value would be. To start, pick a value and ask yourself, "If I were doing things that allowed me to live up to this value, what exactly would I be doing?" For example, if you value taking care of your health, does that mean that you would be preparing home-cooked meals, working out three times a week, and brushing and flossing daily? If your value is to learn something new every day, does that mean you'd be reading the daily paper, listening to a specific television or radio program, and reading a journal related to your field of work? Literally, what will you be doing if you are fulfilling that value? You may have few values or many—the number doesn't matter. What's important is identifying the different activities you do and values they represent. You may want to write the list on a new piece of paper.

6. Next, prioritize your values. You may find that some are hard to place as more important or less, but try to get an approximate ranking.

7. Now, on a new sheet of paper, create a wheel with you as the hub and one spoke going out of the hub for each value you identified. (Don't draw the outer ring that represents the wheel just yet.) The spokes should all be the same length. At the end of each spoke, write down the value it represents. Each value should have its own spoke.

8. Now draw lines on each spoke that divide it into equally sized divisions, like you would see on a ruler. Each spoke should have ten divisions.

9. Next, rate the degree of effort you are putting into fulfilling each value, with 0 being none, 10 being very excessive, and 5 being the ideal amount of effort. The "ideal" amount of effort will vary depending on how important that value is to you. For example, suppose you value "career advancement" more than "maintaining friendships." If that's the case, the ideal amount of effort for career advancement will be a lot (maybe 60 hours a week), and the ideal amount for maintaining friendships will be less (maybe 5 hours a week). Remember, the ideal amount of energy is represented by the number 5—not the number 10. It's possible to put *too much* effort into one value, and that's what you're recording when you rate it above a 5. For instance, you may value a good work ethic, but if you're spending 70 hours a week at your job and other things are suffering as a result, that's *too* much effort, and you might rate it at a 9 or 10. Look back at the list of things you did over the past week, and decide how much effort you spent on each value. Put a dot on the rung of the spoke to represent the amount of effort you put into fulfilling that value this week.

10. Now draw a line to connect the dots. This will reveal the balance. A perfect 5 in each value will make for a smooth-run-

ning wheel, but for most of us, there will be too little or too much effort going into each value. A spiky wheel shows where you can cut back or increase effort to improve balance in your life.

11. Finally, note the ways you can decrease or increase your effort on any of the out-of-balance spokes. To figure out the exact change you want to make, ask, "What do I need to start doing or stop doing to achieve the ideal of a balanced life?"

PSYCHOTROPIC MEDICATIONS

ALTHOUGH MANY people with anxiety and mild to moderate depression do well with psychotherapy alone, there are cases in which the treatment will be aided by medication. Therefore, it is useful to have a general idea of what medications can do, when you should recommend them, and when it is time to discontinue them.

How do you know when to recommend that a client consider medication? With co-occurring anxiety and depression, the biggest challenge is balancing the low energy and the intense physical arousal of anxiety. If severe symptoms of either depression or anxiety continue to persist over many sessions, medication may be needed to help achieve better balance so that psychotherapy can do its work.

With depression, medication may help if:

- Clients express a desire to try techniques or make lifestyle changes but from week to week make no progress or do not demonstrate effort between sessions.

- Clients complain of fatigue, find it hard to get out of bed, and muster only enough energy for basic daily functions.
- Clients have trouble concentrating. This will interfere with many aspects of cognitive therapy and may affect memory as well.
- Clients experience physical aches and pains that are disruptive but vague and unconnected to a physical disorder.

With anxiety, medication may help if:
- Clients are suffering intensely ruminative, negative, or fearful thoughts.
- Clients are unable to push aside ruminating worry even when they must pay attention to something else, or, if they *are* able to briefly suspend ruminating, they find themselves worrying again the minute they have nothing else to hold their attention.
- Clients' panic attacks are as frequent as a few times a week or more.
- Clients complain of feeling "bad" all the time. (Ask if it feels like dread without a specific thing they are dreading.) This level of distress is hard to control at first without medication, and it interferes with any good feeling or experience that might improve the comorbid depression.
- Socially anxious clients have strong physical signs (flushing, shaky legs, quivering voice, palpitating heart), especially in ordinary social circumstances such as when walking out of a meeting or a theater, speaking at a meeting, or ordering food at a restaurant.
- Clients cannot calm down and feel terrified at the thought of being in social situations such as parties or at busy public places like a shopping mall. In these cases, calming down is

an essential component of making therapy work, and medication may be needed to achieve that.

WHAT MEDICATIONS ARE HELPFUL?

Because I am not trained as a prescriber, I couch all my remarks about medication to clients in general terms and do not make specific recommendations about whether a drug or a dose is right for them. Instead, I help them formulate questions for their prescriber that will help them make the right choices—whether that choice is to start a medication, switch medications, change dosage, or wean off medications. Knowing which medications are most often used for anxiety and depression, and how they work, will help you guide your clients in asking their prescribers the right questions.

Selective Serotonin Reuptake Inhibitors

Selective serotonin reuptake inhibitors (SSRIs) are intended to make the neurotransmitter serotonin more available in your brain. They are not mood-altering in that they don't give a person immediate relief from depression. Therefore they are not addictive. These medications help your brain increase its production of serotonin by blocking the return of serotonin molecules into the cell that released them. When the cell that releases serotonin does not pick any back up from the synapse between cells, it gets a message that there is not enough serotonin, and the brain goes to work to make more. SSRIs also contribute to the production of new brain cells that will produce serotonin. For reasons that are not entirely clear, they stimulate a substance called BDNF, which encourages the growth of new brain cells.

Even though SSRIs do have a very small impact on serotonin availability right away, it usually takes weeks for the brain to start producing enough additional serotonin neurotransmitters to change depression. It takes *months* for the brain to maintain that level of production without the medication, and it requires nutrients to build new cells and adequate sleep during that time to produce the serotonin. People taking SSRIs should expect to be on these medications for some time, typically for a year or more. SSRIs should be discontinued only under the supervision of a doctor.

The commonly prescribed SSRIs are:

citalopram (Celexa)
escitalopram (Lexapro)
fluoxetine (Prozac)
fluvoxamine (Luvox)
paroxetine (Paxil)
sertraline (Zoloft)
vilazodone (Viibryd)

Vilazodone is the newest SSRI and it also acts as a partial serotonin agonist.

Serotonin and Norepinephrine Reuptake Inhibitors

Serotonin and norepinephrine reuptake inhibitors (SNRIs) affect both serotonin and norepinephrine simultaneously. SNRIs include:

desvenlafaxine (Pristiq)
duloxetine (Cymbalta)
venlafaxine (Effexor)

Tricyclic Antidepressants

These medications are older drugs and have been largely replaced as the first choice for antidepressant treatment. They work similarly to the SSRIs and SNRIs, blocking reuptake of serotonin, norepinephrine, and dopamine. However, because they are less selective, they tend to have more side effects than newer medications and are more risky in potential for overdose. They are effective, though, and may be prescribed in specific situations. The tricyclic antidepressants include:

amitriptyline (Elavil, Endep)
amoxapine (Asendin)
clomipramine (Anafranil)
desipramine (Norpramin)
doxepin (Sinequan)
imipramine (Tofranil)
maprotiline (Ludiomil)
nortriptyline (Pamelor, Aventyl)
protriptyline (Vivactil)
trimipramine (Surmontil)

Monoamine Oxidase Inhibitors

Monoamine oxidase inhibitors (MAOIs) are antidepressants that slow down the action of the enzyme that clears neurotransmitters from the synapses. This means there is more opportunity for the necessary neurotransmitters to be received after they are released. Because MAOIs have potential for dangerous side effects when taken in combination with foods that contain tyramine, dietary precautions must be followed carefully. This is one significant reason why these medications are less frequently prescribed. MAOIs include:

phenelzine (Nardil)
tranylcypromine (Parnate)
isocarboxazid (Marplan)
selegiline (Emsam; available as a transdermal patch)

Benzodiazepines

Benzodiazepines are prescribed for anxiety symptoms, such as intense nervousness or panic attacks. The benzodiazepines work on GABA, a neurotransmitter that slows firing between brain cells. The calming effects of benzodiazepines work quickly, usually within 30 to 60 minutes, and last for several hours, depending on the type of drug prescribed. That is why they are considered mood-altering. Typically a physician will prescribe this drug for a brief period of time—weeks, not months.

Benzodiazepines are contraindicated in treatment for:

- People with active or past alcohol or drug addiction. Due to their addictive potential, these drugs could reinforce the addictive habit or prompt relapse. However, there may be unusual situations in which benzodiazepines could be necessary, with carefully monitored use of the medication.
- Very young patients who have not completed puberty, because they are more likely to have paradoxical reactions.
- The elderly, who are often using other medications. Use of other medications increases the risk of drug interactions; also, benzodiazepines increase the risk of dizziness, falling, and memory problems.

Benzodiazepines work best to decrease the high degree of physical arousal that goes with intense feelings of stress or agitation. Typically they are prescribed in tandem with an SSRI for the first few weeks on that medication. In some cases they are prescribed to be used as needed in specific, planned-for situations in which it is desirable to minimize intense arousal. Benzodiazepines should not be discontinued abruptly, as this can cause unpleasant or serious effects, depending on the length of time the drugs have been used. The most commonly prescribed benzodiazepines include:

alprazolam (Xanax)
clonazepam (Klonopin)
lorazepam (Ativan)

Buspirone

Buspirone (BuSpar) is an atypical anti-anxiety drug in the class of medications called "azapirones." Azapirones work on the serotonin system, but differently than the SSRIs. They cause neurons to release more serotonin whenever they fire, and thus a little more serotonin is available to affect all the systems where it is active. Buspirone has some impact on the dopamine system, and is more likely to "take the edge off" of the kind of agitation that besets those with comorbid depression and anxiety. It does not work immediately, but rather takes several days to a few weeks. This is a medication that someone with generalized anxiety and depression might benefit from using for a period of months.

Bupropion

Bupropion (Wellbutrin, Zyban) selectively raises levels of dopamine in the brain. Because dopamine affects attention and feelings of reward, bupropion works particularly well to raise energy and help people feel more interest in life. It is very helpful for people who are lethargic or disinterested, as might be seen in both depression and social anxiety.

COMMON PSYCHOTROPIC TREATMENTS
FOR THE SEVEN CLIENT TYPES

As I mentioned earlier, because I am not trained as a prescriber, I do not make medication recommendations, and the following sections should not be read as such. However, I have found that certain medications seem to work well for certain client types.

The Low-Energy Client

Low-energy clients often do well on SSRIs and bupropion. The typical pattern of prescription is long-term use of these two medications to improve both mood and energy.

The Hopeless Ruminator

Hopeless ruminators are likely to benefit most from the SSRIs. Their rumination is more often born of depression than of anxiety and therefore these clients typically do not need the anti-anxiety effects of other medications.

The Panicky & Depressed Client

For panicky and depressed clients, SSRIs along with short-term use of a benzodiazepine (about 3 weeks followed by a week of gradually reducing the dose until cessation) can reduce the sensitivity of the brain and thus decrease panic attacks. It takes a few weeks for the full therapeutic effects of the SSRIs to take hold, but the immediate action of the benzodiazepine will decrease panic immediately. After weaning off the benzodiazepine, the frequency of panic should be somewhat less. It is quite common for these clients to have a prescription for a benzodiazepine taken on an as-needed basis when they panic. These drugs do not stop the panic attack itself, but they minimize the very uncomfortable aftereffects of an attack—the shakiness and feelings of dread.

The Worried & Exhausted Client

These clients may need SSRI or SNRI medication and often benefit from appropriate supplements (discussed later in the chapter). Their recovery is slower than that of most clients due to the long-term depletion they have often suffered.

The Quiet Avoider

Quiet avoiders often benefit from bupropion to raise their level of interest and motivation. Trying new behavior requires a measure of interest and the ability to feel reward, both of which this drug will help with.

The High-Energy Anxious & Depressed Client

These clients may be most in need of an SSRI and buspirone because they find it very hard to interrupt rumination. The combination of negativity and a highly active brain makes for intense worrying, and while clients are learning to adapt their lifestyles and manage their cognitions, these medications can provide relief. High-energy anxious and depressed clients may need longer-term anxiety treatment, making buspirone a better choice than the addictive benzodiazepines, which should be used only for short durations or on an as-needed basis.

The High-Anxiety Client

This client is often the most likely to benefit from benzodiazepine use and least likely to want to take it. Physicians often prescribe SSRIs plus benzodiazepines to start, as for panicky and depressed clients, and then discontinue the benzodiazepine. A benefit to the high-energy client is the improved sleep that benzodiazepines promote (although these medications are not typically considered sleep medications). The brains is quieted enough to stop the worry dreaming and the light and restless sleep pattern. As clients sleep better, their mood and cognition improve as well.

COMPLICATED SITUATIONS

A person with depression and anxiety may well have other problems complicating treatment with medication. When more than one condition is present, psychiatrists are best equipped to identify and prescribe the combination of medications that will stabilize all the aspects of the comorbid conditions.

INSOMNIA

Insomnia is common in people with co-occurring depression and anxiety. Usually medication will resolve that problem over time, as long as the person practices good sleep hygiene. However, there are many causes of insomnia—including some medical conditions, such as sleep apnea, that require appropriate diagnosis and medical treatment. In depression, debilitating insomnia may require a short-term use of sleep medication, but the type of insomnia will affect the choice of medication. Medications vary widely in the way they affect sleep onset and the quality of sleep.

AGE-RELATED CONCERNS

The age of the patient is an important consideration in medication. Although many people are reluctant to medicate a child, severe depression and anxiety will have an impact on the child's development. The SSRIs fluoxetine (Prozac) and escitalopram (Lexapro) have been approved by the FDA for use in children. Another concern is the possibility of attention deficit disorder (ADD). Especially into adolescence and young adulthood, if ADD has not been correctly diagnosed or treated, the condition can contribute to depression, as low self-esteem, mistakes, social errors, and failure to achieve commensurate with ability can be very discouraging and those deficits accrue over time. Treating the ADD will improve any comorbid depression.

Age-related issues in geriatric patients include comorbid physical conditions in which medication or the outcome of the disease produces depression. Also, if a geriatric patient presents with mental distraction or confusion, it is important to differentiate dementia and depression. Treating with an antidepressant medication alone may not be enough.

OTHER ISSUES

In the previously mentioned situations and many others, other types of drugs may augment antidepressant treatment to decrease anxiety, improve thought clarity and mood stability, and so on. For example, a person with bipolar disorder will require medications that stabilize the mood or that control both depression and mania, and finding the right medication is a process that involves careful appraisal of the rapidity of the cycle, the severity of the symptoms, and the person's response to the medication.

Because there many complex individual situations, it is best to consult a psychiatrist. Psychiatrists have specialized training to know:

• How psychotropic medications affect people at different ages
• How psychotropic medications affect people with different symptom expressions

- What medications work best for people with complicated depression or comorbid mental-health conditions
- New options for medication or augmenting medication

It is well worth a visit to a psychiatrist to get medication right. For a more thorough discussion of medications that are used for mental-health treatment, see Stephen Sobel's *Successful Psychopharmacology*, in the References at the end of this book.

HERBAL AND SUPPLEMENTAL OPTIONS FOR BRAIN HEALTH

There is abundant evidence that you can improve your mood, create a healthier brain and body, and revitalize your health by what you eat, what kinds of supplements you add to your diet, and how you deliberately employ physical exercise. If you are interested in how the brain uses nutrients to manufacture neurotransmitters and how to better balance those nutrients, consult the section on nutrition and supplements in the Reading & Resources at the end of this book. There you will find some excellent resources, such as *How to use Herbs, Nutrients & Yoga in Mental Health Care* (Brown, Gerbarg, & Muskin, 2009) and *Potatoes, Not Prozac* (DesMaisons, 1998).

A FINAL NOTE

Medication may help, but it can't teach clients the techniques that will help them use their brain to change their brain. By learning and practicing the tools offered in this book, clients can learn how to manage their depression and anxiety symptoms, whether they decide to pair that treatment with medication or not.

Reading & Resources

The Brain and Methods to Work With It

Amen, D., & Routh, L. (2004). *Healing anxiety and depression.* New York: Penguin.

Walsh, D., & Bennett, N. (2004). *Why do they act that way? A survival guide to the adolescent brain for you and your teen.* New York: Free Press.

Wehrenberg, M., & Prinz, S. (2007). *The anxious brain.* New York: Norton.

Listening to Your Body

Childre, D., & Martin, H. (1999). *The heartmath solution.* San Francisco: HarperCollins.

Cornell, A. (2013). *Focusing in clinical practice: The essence of change.* New York: Norton.

Cornell, A. W. (1996). *The power of focusing.* Oakland, CA: New Harbinger.

Gendlin, E. (1998). *Focusing-oriented psychotherapy.* New York: Guilford.

The following websites offer devices for biofeedback and handheld or computer-based devices to improve physical and psychological wellbeing:

www.eegspectrum.com
www.heartmath.com

www.wilddivine.com
www.stresseraser.com

Worksheets and Activities for Social Skills, Assertiveness, and Anger Management

Brennan, I. (2011). *Anger antidotes: How not to lose your s#&!.* New York: Norton.

Carter, L., & Minirth, F. (1993). *The anger workbook.* Wheaton, IL: Thomas Nelson.

Cooper, B., & Widdows, N. (2008). *Social success workbook for teens.* Oakland, CA: Instant Help Books.

Eifert, G., McKay, M., & Forsyth, J. (2005). *Acceptance and commitment therapy for anxiety disorders.* Oakland, CA: New Harbinger.

Eifert, G., McKay, M., & Forsyth, J. (2006). *ACT on life not on anger.* Oakland, CA: New Harbinger.

Khalsa, S. (1996). *Group exercise for enhancing social skills and self-esteem.* Sarasota, FL: Professional Resource Press.

Madson, P. R. (2005). *Improv wisdom.* New York: Crown.

Myles, B., Trautman, M., & Schelvan, R. (2004). *The hidden curriculum.* Shawnee Mission, KS: Autism Asperger Publishing Company.

Nay, W. R. (2012) *Taking charge of anger* (2nd ed.). New York: Guilford.

Novotni, M. (1999). *What does everybody else know that I don't know?* Plantation, FL: Specialty Press.

O'Hanlon, B. (1999). *Do one thing different.* New York: William Morrow.

Robbins, J. M. (2002). *Acting techniques in everyday life.* New York: Marlowe.

Seigel, D., & Hartzell, M. (2003). *Parenting from the inside out.* New York: Putnam.

Wilson, B., & DeMaria, R. (2009). *He's just no good for you: A guide to getting out of a destructive relationship.* Guilford, CT: GPP Life.

Zeff, T., & Aron, E. (2004). *The highly sensitive person's survival guide: Essential skills for living well in an overstimulating world.* Oakland, CA: New Harbinger.

Relaxation, Meditation

Brantley, J., Millstine, W., & Matik, W. (2007). *Five good minutes: 100 mindful practices to help you relieve stress and bring your best to work.* Oakland, CA: New Harbinger.

Davis, M., Eschelman, E., & McKay, M. (2008). *The relaxation and stress reduction workbook.* New Harbinger: California.

Ensley, E. (2007). *Prayer that relieves stress and worry.* North Carolina: Contemplative Press.
Hanh, T. N. (1999). *The miracle of mindfulness.* Boston: Beacon.
Newberg, A., & Waldman, M. (2009). *How God changes your brain.* New York: Ballantine.

Nutrition and Supplements

Brown, R., Gerbarg, P., & Muskin, P. (2009). *How to use herbs, nutrients & yoga in mental health care.* New York: Norton.
DesMaisons, K. (1998). *Potatoes, not Prozac.* New York: Simon & Schuster.
Hendler, S., & Rovik, M. S. (Eds.). (2001). *Physician's desk reference for nutritional supplements.* Des Moines, IA: Thompson Healthcare.
Henslin, E. (2008). *This is your brain on joy.* Nashville, TN: Thomas Nelson.
Northrup, C. (2010). *The wisdom of menopause.* New York: Bantam.
Northrup, C. (2012). *Women's bodies, women's wisdom.* New York: Bantam.
Weil, A. (2000). *Eating well for optimal health.* New York: Knopf.

Therapy

Baker, D. (2004). *What happy people know.* New York: St. Martins-Griffin.
Burns, D. (1999). *The feeling good handbook.* New York: Plume.
Ecker, B., & Hully, L. (2007). *Coherence therapy manual.* Available at: www.dobt.com
Gallo, F., & Vincenzi, H. (2000). *Energy tapping.* Oakland, CA: New Harbinger.
McMullin, R. (2005). *Taking out your mental trash.* New York: Norton.
Pratt, G., & Lambrou, P. (2000). *Instant emotional healing.* New York: Random House.
Shapiro, F. (2001). *Eye movement desensitization and reprocessing: Basic principles, protocols, and procedures* (2nd ed.). New York: Guilford.

Anxiety and Depression Organizations

American Psychiatric Association
www.psych.org

American Psychological Association
www.apa.org

Anxiety and Depression Association of America
www.adaa.org

Anxiety Disorder Association of America
www.adaa.org

Children and Adults with Hyperactivity Disorder
www.chadd.org

The Depression and Bipolar Support Alliance
www.dbsalliance.org

National Institute of Mental Health
www.nimh.nih.gov

Obsessive-Compulsive Foundation
www.ocfoundation.org

Assessment Tools

Self-Assessment
Myers-Briggs Type Indicator
www.MBTIcomplete.com

Freudenberger, H., and North, G. (1985). *Women's burnout.* New York: Doubleday.
Neff, K. (2011). *Self-compassion: Stop beating yourself up and leave insecurity behind.* New York: William Morrow.

Rotter Locus of Control
www.psychologytoday.tests.psychtests.com/take_test.php?idRegTest=1317
www.psych.uncc.edu/pagoolka/LC.html

Self-Compassion
www.self-compassion.org (scales for researchers and a self-compassion test for personal assessment)

Burnout and Vigor
www.shirom.org (for scales on burnout and vigor)

Assessment Resources for Clinicians

Autism Diagnostic Observation Schedule (a semi-structured interview especially useful for previously undiagnosed adults with serious mental illness)

Beck Depression and Beck Anxiety Scales (available for purchase from www. pearsonassessments.com)

Hamilton Depression and Anxiety Scales (available from several sites on the Internet)

The Positive and Negative Affect Schedule (a 20-item self-report measure that helps differentiate anxiety from depression)

Resources to Assess Children and Adolescents

American Academy of Child and Adolescent Psychiatry
www.aacap.org

Massachusetts General Hospital (for screening tools for children and adolescents)
www.massgeneral.org/schoolpsychiatry/screeningtools_table.asp

For information on Aperger's and autism:
www.autism-society.org
www.usautism.org

The following scales can be ordered online:
Anxiety Sensitivity Index (ASI)
Children's Depression Index (CDI)
Multidimensional Anxiety Scale for Children (MASC) or MASC–10.
Revised Children's Manifest Anxiety Scale (RC-MAS)
Pre-School Age Psychiatric Assessment (PAPA)
The Positive and Negative Affect Schedule (PANAS)
Screen for Child Anxiety Related Emotional Disorders (SCARED)

Herbal Medicine and Supplements

For an impressive list of resources, websites, and groups that study and promote herbal remedies, see the University of Pittsburgh website:

www.pitt.edu/~cbw/herb.html
Medline offers a variety of nutritional and alternative medicine treatments:
www.medlineplus.gov

The American Botanical Council is another resource:
www.abc.herbalgram.org

Three commercial sites, whose products I am not recommending, have impressive educational information about health issues and supplementation:
www.drweil.com
www.lef.org
www.mercola.com

Guided Imagery and Relaxation Audio CDs

Belleruth Naparstak
www.healthjourneys.com

Margaret Wehrenberg
www.margaretwehrenberg.com

Sleep

American Academy of Sleep Medicine
www.aasmnet.org
www.sleepeducation.com

Other Therapies

EMDR International Association
5806 Mesa Drive, Suite 360
Austin, Texas 78731
866-451-5200
Email: info@emdria.org

Emotional Freedom Technique
PO Box 269
Coulterville, CA 95311
www.emofree.com

Energy Tapping
www.energypsych.com

Instant Emotional Healing
www.instantemotionalhealing.com

Medication

National Alliance on Mental Illness (for information on mental illnesses and
a list of resources for people who cannot afford medication or who do not
have insurance)

NAMI
Colonial Place Three
2107 Wilson Blvd., Suite 300
Arlington, VA 22201
1-800-950-NAMI
www.nami.org/Template.cfm?section=about_medications&Template=/
ContentManagement/contentDisplay.cfm&ContentID=19169

Addictions

National Institute of Drug Addiction
www.nida.nih.gov

National Clearinghouse on Drug and Alcohol Addiction
1-800-729-6686

Addiction Self-Help
www.alcoholics-anonymous.org
www.rational.org
www.smartrecovery.org
www.ca.org

Family Help With Addiction
http://www.al-anon.alateen.org
http://www.familiesanonymous.org

Trauma

International Society for Traumatic Stress Studies
60 Revere Drive, Suite 500
Northbrook, IL 60062
847-480-9028
    Email: istss@istss.org

Sidran Traumatic Stress Foundation
200 E. Joppa Road, Suite 207
Baltimore, MD 21286
410-825-8888
    www.sidran.org

International Critical Incident Stress Foundation
10176 Baltimore National Pike, Unit 201
Ellicott City, MD 21042
410-750-9600
    www.icisf.org

References

American Psychiatric Association. (2013). *Diagnostic and statistical manual of mental disorders* (5th ed.). Washington, DC: Author.

Bergmann, U. (1998). Speculations on the neurobiology of EMDR. *Traumatology, 4,* 4–16.

Black, C. (2009). *It will never happen to me.* Center City, MN: Hazelden.

Cohen, S., Janicki-Deverts, D., Doyle, W., Miller, G., Frank, E., Rabin, B., et al. (2012). Chronic stress, glucocorticoid receptor resistance, inflammation, and disease risk. *Proceedings of the National Academy of Sciences,* April 12.

Craske, M. (2012). The R-doc initiative: Science and practice. *Depression and Anxiety, 29,* 253–256.

Eisenberger, N. I., Taylor, S. E., Gable, S. L., Hilmert, C. J., & Lieberman, M. D. (2007). Neural pathways link social support to attenuated neuroendocrine stress responses. *Neuroimage, 35*(4), 1601–1612.

Elovainio, M., Jokela, M., Kivimaki, M., Pulkki-Raback, L., Lehtimaki, T., Airla, N., et al. (2007). Genetic variants in the DRD2 gene moderate the relationship between stressful life events and depressive symptoms in adults: Cardiovascular risk in young Finns study. *Psychosomatic Medicine, 69,* 391–395.

Farchione, T. J., Fairholme, C. P., Ellard, K. K., Boisseau, C. L., Thompson-Hollands, J., Carl, J. R., et al. (2012). Unified protocol for transdiagnostic treatment of emotional disorders: A randomized controlled trial. *Behavior Therapy, 45,* 666–678.

Felitti, V., Anda, R., Nordenberg, D., Williamson, D., Spitz. A., Edwards, V., et al. (1998). The relationship of adult health status to childhood abuse and household dysfunction. *American Journal of Preventive Medicine, 14*, 245–258.

Fredrickson, B. L. (2001). The role of positive emotions in positive psychology: The broaden-and-build theory of positive emotions. *American Psychologist, 56*, 218–226.

Kendler, K., Thornton, L., & Gardner C. (2001). Genetic risk, number of previous depressive episodes, and stressful life events in predicting onset of major depression. *American Journal of Psychiatry, 158*(4), 582–586.

Lazarus, A. (1981). *The practice of multi-modal therapy*. New York: McGraw-Hill.

Munago, M. (2012). The serotonin transporter gene and depression. *Depression and Anxiety, 29*, 915–917.

Naparstek, B. (2000). *What is guided imagery?* Retrieved August 23, 2013, from http://www.healthjourneys.com/what_is_guided_imagery.asp

Nemeroff, C. B. (2004). Neurobiological consequences of childhood trauma. *Journal of Clinical Psychiatry, 65*(supp. 11), 18–28.

Palmer, S., Woolfe, R. (Eds.). (2000). *Integrative and eclectic counselling and psychotherapy*. London: Sage.

Schore, A. (2003). *Affect dysregulation and repair of the self.* New York: Norton.

Siegel, D., & Hartzell, M. (2003). *Parenting from the inside out*. New York: Putnam.

Shelton, R. (2007). The molecular neurobiology of depression. *Psychiatry Clinics of North America, 30*(1), 1–11.

Siddique, J., Chung, J. Y., Brown, C. H., & Miranda, J. (2012). Comparative effectiveness of medication versus cognitive-behavioral therapy in a randomized controlled trial of low-income young minority women with depression. *Journal of Consulting and Clinical Psychology, 80*, 995–1006.

Sobel, S. (2012). *Successful psychopharmacology*. New York: Norton.

Taylor, S. E. (2011). How psychosocial resources enhance health and well-being. In S. Donaldson, M. Csikszentmihalyi, & J. Nakamura (Eds.), *Applied positive psychology: Improving everyday life, health, schools, work, and society*. New York: Routledge.

Wiles, N., Thomas, L., Abel, A., Ridgway, N., Turner, N., Campbell, J., et al. (2013). Cognitive behavioural therapy as an adjunct to pharmacotherapy for primary care based patients with treatment resistant depression: Results of the CoBalT randomised controlled trial. *Lancet, 381*, 375–84.

Yehuda, R. (1997). Stress and glucocorticoid. *Science, 275*, 1662–1663.

Yehuda, R., Harvey, P., Buschbaum, M., Tischler, L., & Schmeidler, J., (2007). Hippocampal volume in aging combat veterans with and without post-traumatic stress disorder: Relation to risk and resilience factors. *Journal of Psychiatric Research, 41*(5), 435–445.

Yehuda, R., & LeDoux, J. (2007). Response variation following trauma: A translational neuroscience approach to understanding PTSD. *Neuron*, 56(1), 19–32.

Zbozinek, T., Rose, R., Wolitzky-Taylor, K., Sherbourne, C., Sullivan, G., Stein, M., et al. (2012). Diagnostic overlap of generalized anxiety disorder and major depressive disorder in a primary care sample. *Depression and Anxiety, 29*, 1065–1071.

Index